NAPOLEON HILL'S
A YEAR OF GROWING RICH

NAPOLEON HILL was born into poverty in 1883, and achieved great success as an attorney and journalist. He was an advisor to Franklin Roosevelt and a confidant of Andrew Carnegie's. In recent years, the Napoleon Hill Foundation has revived his writings, winning him an immense international audience for such books as *Think and Grow Rich, Think and Grow Rich Action Pack* (Plume), and *Succeed and Grow Rich Through Persuasion* (Signet).

It Takes Only Minutes Each Week to
Reap a Lifetime of Rewards

Wealth, power, health, happiness, and fulfillment depend on one person—yourself.

Now Napoleon Hill, a bestselling author and timeless millionaire-making wise man, offers you the one and only tool you will ever need to be all you want to be, do all you want to do, and have all you want to have.

Here, in his inspiring and empowering work, you will find a message for each week of the year that will let you see yourself and the world around you in a dazzling new way. You will learn to realize all the strengths within you and spot the vast wealth of opportunities at yo ger-tips even as you take in these words. Let N ll's weekly meditations help you reap * y have seemed beyond your d within your grasp.

NAPOLEON HILL'S A YEAR OF GROWING RICH

FIFTY-TWO STEPS TO ACHIEVING LIFE'S REWARDS

Napoleon Hill

Foreword by W. Clement Stone
Edited by Matthew Sartwell

*Anthology Assembled by
Samuel A. Cypert*

A TarcherPerigee Book

tarcherperigee

An imprint of Penguin Random House LLC
375 Hudson Street
New York, New York 10014

First published by Plume, a member of Penguin Group (USA) Inc., 1993
Published with the Green preface 2007
This edition published 2016

The articles in this book first appeared in *Success Unlimited* magazine.

Tarcher and Perigee are registered trademarks, and the colophon is a trademark of Penguin Random House LLC.

Most TarcherPerigee books are available at special quantity discounts for bulk purchase for sales promotions, premiums, fund-raising, and educational needs. Special books or book excerpts also can be created to fit specific needs. For details, write: SpecialMarkets@penguinrandomhouse.com.

The Library of Congress has cataloged the Plume edition as follows:
Hill, Napoleon, 1883–1970
[Year of growing rich]
Napoleon Hill's a year of growing rich : fifty-two steps to achieving life's rewards / by Napoleon Hill ; foreword by W. Clement Stone ; edited by Matthew Sartwell ; anthology assembled by Samuel A. Cypert.
p. cm.
A collection of essays originally published in the magazine Success Unlimited.
Includes index.
ISBN 9780452270541 (pbk.)
1. Success in business. 2. Optimism. 3. Attitude (Psychology)
I. Sartwell, Matthew. II. Cypert, Samuel A. III. Title. HF5386.H577 1993
650.14—dc20   93-4361

Printed in the United States of America
47   46   45   44   43   42   41   40   39

Contents

Preface   ix

Foreword by W. Clement Stone   xii

Introduction   xiii

WEEK
1   No One Drifts to Success   1
2   Learn How to Live Your Own Life   4
3   Motivate Yourself to Achieve Success   7
4   Some Succeed, Others Fail ... Why?   10
5   Strength Grows Out of Struggle   13
6   Sincerity   16
7   Hopefulness   19
8   Patience   22
9   Flexibility   25
10 Enthusiasm   27
11 Use Your Personal Magnetism   31
12 Have Confidence in Yourself   33
13 Strengthen Your Sense of Humor   36
14 Showmanship   38
15 Choose Your Goal   40

Contents

16 Use Your Personal Initiative   43
17 Get the Job You Want   46
18 Get a Promotion   49
19 How One Man Won a Promotion   52
20 Lend a Helping Hand   54
21 Live Harmoniously with Others   57
22 Let Others Help You Achieve Success   60
23 Welcome Help from Others   62
24 Work with Your Team   65
25 Humility   68
26 Sell to Yourself   71
27 Wake Up and Meet Your Positive Self   75
28 The Power of Mental Attitude   78
29 Keep a Positive Mental Attitude   81
30 Be Optimistic   83
31 Control Your Mental Attitude   86
32 The Value of Positive Thinking   89
33 Let Habits Work for You   92
34 Think Accurately   95
35 Cultivate Creative Vision   98
36 Concentration   101
37 Progress Calls for an Open Mind   103
38 The Blessings of Failure   106
39 Learn from Defeat   109
40 Overcome Fear to Reach Your Goal   112
41 Discipline Yourself for Success   114
42 Stop Making Failures of Our Children   117
43 Sorrow Can Be a Blessing   120
44 Look in the Mirror   123

Contents

45	Your Source of Power	126
46	Use the Unbeatable Master	129
47	Give Thanks Every Day	132
48	Help in Achieving Peace of Mind	135
49	Contentment	138
50	Not Too Much, Not Too Little	140
51	Does This Picture Fit You?	143
52	The Power of Faith	145
	Index	149

Preface

The writings of Napoleon Hill are designed in such a manner that you can read and study one section per week for a year to help you improve achievement in your financial and personal life. Do not judge the book's small size until you have the opportunity to become familiar with the contents. You can expect to learn from the material and be inspired with each lesson.

Some of the articles will have more meaning to readers than others. It will depend on each reader's particular circumstances and desires.

While Lesson 16 is only three pages in this small book, it literally jumped out at me as a reminder of the reason so many people do not truly succeed in life.

Personal initiative is very important if you wish to rise above the crowd. Personal initiative simply means that you will do the thing you ought to do without someone else telling you to do it. Napoleon Hill—eighty-five years ago—in his own magazine wrote an article that shows how personal initiative worked for a young lad—he being that person.

I found that personal initiative was of great appeal to

me because I recognized the benefit from this lesson. I spent thirty-eight years in banking and finance and was president and CEO of a bank at the age of forty-one. Even today as executive director of the Napoleon Hill Foundation and having the responsibility to see that Napoleon Hill's books and philosophy of success are spread throughout the world, I have a sign on my desk to remind me of this lesson on initiative that simply says, *If it is to be It is up to me.* The message is a daily reminder that personal initiative is necessary if excellent results are to be expected.

A Year of Growing Rich is exactly what it says—lessons to help you achieve your goals in life.

Somewhere among the fifty-two articles, you may find some that have little appeal to you. Some lessons may be easier while some may be more difficult and require more concentration and effort.

Lesson 38: "The Blessings of Failure" can require more of a challenge on the student's part if maximum results are to be achieved. For example, the viewpoint you take of failure can make all the difference in the world as to whether you have success in life or become bitter—a whiner who cannot accept responsibility. Failure should be looked upon as a lesson learned. This lesson alone shows that the majority of people will not be successful because they quit at the first sign of failure. Persistence is the quality that must be learned if success is your goal. Along with your lessons, read the biographies of great men and women who have overcome difficulties. The stories of Abraham Lincoln, Booker T. Washington, and Wilma Randolph tell of three great Americans who succeeded in spite of adversities when most people would have simply quit.

I suggest you pay great attention to Lesson 33: "Let Habits Work for You." We are ruled by habits; it has been said that we make our habits, then our habits make us. Habits are choices that one makes and repeats over and over until the habits become so much a part of us that they are more or less automatic; we do them with little thought.

Once you have completed Napoleon Hill's *A Year of Growing Rich*, go back to the beginning and evaluate yourself on each lesson. No doubt you will be pleased with the progress you have made on some, and with others you will probably decide that further studying and applications will be necessary to help you along the road to success.

Remember: Reading, studying, and applying the lessons will be revealed to you when you look in the mirror. Like money left in a bank account, the book will continue to pay dividends throughout your life.

—Don M. Green
Executive Director
Napoleon Hill Foundation

Foreword

It was my good fortune to serve as Napoleon Hill's general manager for a ten-year period back in the 1950s and '60s. During the time we were associated, our lectures, books, movies and personal consultations achieved gratifying, effective and often amazing results. Dr. Hill and I taught thousands of individuals to motivate themselves and others—at will—to acquire the true riches of life as well as to achieve incredible financial and business success.

We soon observed, however, that many people learned the principles but did not develop the *habit of applying them*. They lost their inspiration, they stopped trying. We then realized that motivation (an inspiration to action) is like a fire: Unless it is constantly refueled, the flame is extinguished.

To keep the motivational flames burning brightly, Dr. Hill and I founded *Success Unlimited* magazine. Through its inspirational articles, we provided unlimited fuel to those who had the desire to motivate themselves to ever higher levels of achievement. It worked marvelously: Thousands of people came to rely upon the little magazine with the big ideas to provide regular infusions of enthusiasm.

The articles included in this anthology first appeared in *Success Unlimited*. Because of their enduring appeal, the Napoleon Hill Foundation has made available this collection of some of Dr. Hill's most popular articles. Like his best-selling book, *Think and Grow Rich*, each article is interesting reading, and each contains a message especially for you. Each is designed to stimulate you to develop the unlimited power of your mind.

This book alone will not bring you happiness, health, power and wealth. But if these things are what you desire, it will help you generate new ideas and help you stay focused on the achievement of your goals. You will recognize new opportunities that were not previously apparent to you. But most important, you will be impelled to follow through with action.

Good health and happiness can be yours. Wealth— you can acquire it. Power—you have it in unlimited quantities within you. But you must decide whether you are willing to pay the price to extract and use the success principles outlined in this book to acquire the true riches of life. The choice is yours, and yours alone.

If you are ready to discover and use the simple universal principles contained in these pages, you can prepare yourself now by determining precisely what you desire to achieve or acquire. When you have specific objectives and long-term, intermediate and immediate goals, you are much more likely to recognize, relate, assimilate and apply the principles and techniques that will help you achieve them.

I can speak about their effectiveness with some authority, for it was their application that allowed me to start my first insurance company with only one hundred dollars and elevated me to the position of chairman of the board of AON Insurance Companies, a multibillion-dollar organization that now operates on four continents. Thousands of our sales representatives, office employees and shareholders are in upper-income brackets today because they practice the principles Dr. Hill wrote about.

During my years as president of Chicago Boys Clubs, I saw the lives of inner-city youths changed for the better through the application of the profound truths contained in this philosophy of personal achievement. And I have seen recidivism reduced among prison inmates who read Dr. Hill's work in books and magazines while they were incarcerated. The principles are timeless; they are just as applicable today as they were when he first published them in *Success Unlimited*.

I have always made it a practice to evaluate my own work and that of others by a single standard: Results are what count. I know from my own experience and the experiences of thousands of readers who have written to me from all over the world that Napoleon Hill's writings have been a powerful influence in bringing happiness, health, power and wealth to those who had a sincere, burning desire to achieve their objectives.

The articles included in this treasury can do the same for you. If you follow the formula that Napoleon Hill outlined, you will discover—as millions of others have already—that truly the only limitations you have are those that you set up in your own mind.

—W. Clement Stone, chairman,
The Napoleon Hill Foundation

Introduction

This collection of Napoleon Hill's work is designed to give you a week-by-week boost in your efforts to achieve both personal and financial success. As W. Clement Stone has so perceptively written in the Foreword, motivation is a fire that must constantly be refueled if it is to continue to burn.

There are fifty-two articles here, one for each week of the year. Read each week's selection every day of that week at a regular time, a time when you will have the opportunity to consider the implications of Napoleon Hill's advice. None of these articles are lengthy; none of them are difficult to grasp. But they are challenging. After editing this anthology and reviewing its contents repeatedly, I can tell you that I am still struck by new inspirations each time I approach it.

In the last week of my work on this volume, I had just finished rereading Week 30, "Be Optimistic," when I recalled a project I had started then set aside as too unlikely. Emboldened, I took it up again that evening, and by morning I had a written proposal. Within a week, I had sold that project for twenty percent more than I had expected to receive. If I had reread "Be Optimistic," again, I'm certain I would have done even better.

You may not experience such immediate benefits from each selection. "Contentment" (Week 49) has a message that is designed to serve you as much this week as it is years from now, a message whose import will grow ever more clear. "Showmanship" (Week 14), on the other hand, should offer you some concrete tips that you can put into action as soon as you lay this book down.

You may also find that a particular article speaks to you with special clarity. Spend a few extra days or a second week with it. *A Year of Growing Rich* is not a race; it's a process designed to help you. You, rather than a calendar, should determine your progress.

But if you don't see the usefulness of an entry the first time you read it, don't jump ahead to the next one. Messages may be subtle, your state of mind unreceptive. Take the time to give each article due consideration. The most difficult task I faced in culling these selections from a much larger group was that every time I looked at an article I had set aside, I saw new insights, new messages. This is also a good reason to begin the cycle of readings once more after you have made your way through *A Year of Growing Rich*. You will have grown much by the time you come upon the articles again; you will find new wisdom and look upon each with a new perspective.

If rereading the same few hundred words each night seems like drudgery, here are some tips to keep the effort fresh:

- Insert yourself and your day's activities into the message of the article. When, for example, you read the injunction in Week 5 to "meet struggle and master it," look to your life and identify struggles you face.
- Read the selection aloud. Actually hearing the message spoken can make you much more sensitive to its implications.
- Work with a partner. Your spouse is an excellent choice, but so too is an officemate, someone in your car pool, or a friend on the phone. Discuss your reactions, or combine this tip with the suggestion above and read the articles to each other.
- Write out the entry in longhand. At first you might be more aware of the effort of writing, but you'll be forced to notice sections you may have previously skipped over. You may also realize how you were reconstructing Napoleon Hill's words to suit your own agenda. Writing out each word will make you acutely aware of what you are being shown.

Set aside any feeling you may have that you are being assigned homework. The only grade you will receive for reading this book will be one that you give yourself. But unlike seventh grade English, the marks you receive in *A Year of Growing Rich* will mean something to you a year, five years, a dozen years or fifty years down the road. Resolve, here and now, to make this book a tool for achieving what you want, and you will achieve it.

M.S.

NAPOLEON HILL'S
A YEAR OF GROWING RICH

No One Drifts
to Success

You don't have to be a futurist or a fortune-teller to be able to predict someone's future. You can do so by asking him or her one simple question: "What is your one *definite purpose* in life—and what plans have you made to attain it?"

If you ask a hundred people that question, ninety-eight of them will answer with something like, "I'd like to make a good living and become as successful as I can." While the answer sounds good on the surface, if you dig a little deeper, you will find a drifter who will never get anything out of life except the leftovers of truly successful people—those who have a definite purpose and a plan for attaining it. To be successful, you must at this moment decide exactly what your goal is and lay out the steps by which you intend to reach it.

Years ago I worked with a fellow named Stuart Austin Wier of Dallas. He was a contributor to a magazine I edited and was just getting by financially. He would probably have remained a starving writer if a story he was writing about an inventor hadn't suddenly inspired him to change his life.

Much to the surprise of those who knew him, he announced that he was giving up journalism and going back to school to become a patent attorney. He wasn't going to be just any patent attorney, he was going to become "the top patent attorney in the United States." He put his plan into action with such fervor that he completed law school in record time.

When he began his practice, he deliberately sought out the toughest cases. Soon his reputation spread throughout the country and his services were in such high demand that even though his fees reached astronomical levels, he was turning away more clients than he accepted.

The person who acts with purpose and a plan attracts opportunities. How can life give you anything if you don't know what you want yourself? How can others help you to succeed if you haven't decided how to get there yourself? Only with definiteness of purpose will you be able to overcome the defeats and adversities that will stand in your way.

One of America's earliest and most successful franchisers was Lee Maranz, a man who knew what he wanted and how to get it. A mechanical engineer, Maranz invented an automatic ice cream freezer that made soft ice cream. He envisioned a chain of ice cream stores from coast to coast and worked out a plan to make his dream become a reality.

He, like many others since, built his own success by helping others achieve theirs. He helped people set up ice cream shops by furnishing construction and design plans, a revolutionary idea at the time. He sold the ice cream machines at cost and made his profit from the sale of the ice cream mix. The result? That chain of stores Maranz was determined to create across the country.

"If you have a strong belief in yourself, in what you are doing, and what you want to do, no adversity is too difficult to overcome," he said.

If you want to achieve success, make today the day you stop drifting. Decide upon a definite goal. Write it down. Commit it to memory. Decide exactly how you plan to achieve it. Then begin by putting the plan into action immediately.

Your future is what you make it. Decide now what it shall be.

Learn How to Live Your Own Life

You will never find peace of mind by allowing other people to live your life for you.

The most profound fact concerning humanity is this: *The Creator gave us the complete, unchallengeable right of prerogative over one thing, and only one thing—our own mind.* It must have been the Creator's purpose to encourage us to live our own lives, to think our own thoughts, without interference from others. Otherwise we would not have been provided with such a clear dominion over our minds.

Simply by exercising this profound prerogative over your own mind and life, you may lift yourself to great heights of achievement in any field of endeavor you choose. Exercising this prerogative is the only real approach to genius. A genius is simply one who has taken full possession of his own mind and directed it toward objectives of his own choosing, without permitting outside influences to discourage or mislead him.

We all know stories about famous people who turned adversity into advantage, who overcame great obstacles to become rich and famous. They are the successful people who converted stumbling blocks into stepping-stones. They become the geniuses of industry, the Henry Fords, the Thomas Edisons, the Andrew Carnegies, and the Wilbur and Orville Wrights.

But there is a far greater number of lesser-known mortals who refuse to accept defeat. They simply refuse to become one of the vast majority who do little more than eke out a living and experience mostly misery, disappointment and failure.

Many years ago, a young army veteran came to see me about a job. He told me he was disillusioned and discouraged; all he wanted out of life was a meal ticket, a place to sleep, and enough to eat.

He had a look in his eyes—a sort of glassy stare—that told me he thought hope was dead. Here was a perfectly capable young man who was willing to settle for practically nothing when I knew very well that if he changed his attitude he could earn a fortune.

There was something about him, an almost hidden spark that prompted me to ask, "How would you like to become a multimillionaire? Why settle for a meager existence when you can just as easily settle for millions?"

"Don't joke with me," he replied. "I'm hungry and I need a job."

"I am not making fun," I replied. "I am dead serious. You can earn millions if you only are willing to use the assets you now have."

"What do you mean, *assets?*" he exclaimed. "I have nothing but the clothes on my back!"

Gradually, over the course of our conversation, I learned that this young man had been a Fuller Brush salesman before he went into the army: While in the service he had done considerable K.P. duty, and had learned to cook rather well. In other words, besides the natural attributes of a healthy body and a potentially positive mind, his total assets consisted of the fact that he could cook food and he could sell.

Generally, of course, neither selling nor cooking will propel a person into the ranks of multimillionaires, but this veteran took himself out of the ordinary walks of life. He was introduced to his own mind and the possibilities that existed when he took control of it.

In the two hours I spent with this young man, I watched him change from a person lost in a sea of despair into a possibility thinker. He did it all with the strength of one idea. "Why don't you use your selling ability to persuade housewives to invite their neighbors over for a home-cooked dinner, then sell them all cookware?"

I advanced him enough money to buy some clothes, and the first outfit of cooking utensils, then turned him loose. During his first week, he cleared nearly $100 selling aluminum cookware. The next week he doubled that amount. Then he began to train other salespeople who worked for him selling the same cookware.

At the end of four years, he was earning more than a million dollars a year and had set in motion a new selling plan that has since evolved into an industry in its own right. When the ties that bind a human mind are broken and a man is introduced to himself—the real self that has no limitations—I fancy that the gates of hell shake with fear and the bells of heaven ring with joy!

Motivate Yourself to Achieve Success

The greatest reward success brings is self-satisfaction. Although we often assume that the accumulation of wealth is the only measure of success, it is but *one* measure. It is an important one to be sure, but true success is marked by the satisfaction of knowing you have done a job and done it well—that you have achieved the goal you set for yourself.

Einstein, for example, never attained great wealth in his lifetime. But could anyone say he was unsuccessful? Einstein reached the top of his profession and changed the world because he knew what he wanted to do and had a plan for achieving it.

How can you motivate yourself to succeed? The answer lies in following the same method Einstein and all other enormously successful people have followed. Develop a burning desire for something that you wish to have in order to reach a greater goal you have set for yourself. Remember, there is a difference between merely wishing for something and deciding definitely that you are going to have it.

Once you have that burning desire, you will develop an intensity of purpose that will allow you to simply brush aside obstacles that seemed insurmountable before. *All things are possible to the person who believes they are possible.*

Set yourself a definite goal in life. Write it down. Commit it to memory. Direct every thought and all your energies to making it come true. Instead of letting momentary setbacks throw you off course, search in them for the seed of an equivalent benefit which can help you get back on track to attaining your goal.

When Henry Ford began work on his first "horseless buggy," less farsighted people—many of his own relatives and neighbors—laughed at him. Some called him a "crazy inventor."

Crazy or not, Ford knew what he wanted—and had a burning desire to achieve it. He also refused to recognize any limitations. Lacking formal education or training as a mechanic, he simply educated himself. Nothing stands in the way of a person determined to reach a life goal.

Ford changed the face of America. His mass-produced automobiles made transportation affordable for the average family and opened up the country. Whole industries grew up around the automobile: Without Ford's "Tin Lizzie," there would have been no need for a network of highways (and the jobs their construction created), service stations, fast-food franchises and motels.

Another perfect example is John Wanamaker who began as a clerk in a Philadelphia retail store. From the beginning he made up his mind he was going to own a similar store someday. When he announced this to his boss, the store owner laughed and said, "Why, John, you don't have enough money to buy an extra suit of clothes, do you?"

"No," Wanamaker said. "But I want a store like this—or even a better one. And I'm going to get it." At the height of his success, Wanamaker owned one of the greatest mercantile establishments the country has ever known.

"I had very little schooling," Wanamaker said years later. "But I acquired the education I needed the same way a locomotive takes on water—I scooped it up as I ran."

Remember, *Whatever the mind of man can conceive and believe, the mind of man can achieve.* The person determined to attain success starts where he stands, making the best of whatever tools he has and acquiring whatever else he needs along the way. Start from wherever you stand—today.

Some Succeed, Others Fail . . . Why?

This question has mystified people since humans first became dissatisfied with cave dwellings and tried to find some way to make life more comfortable. Perhaps the following comparisons between the characteristics of a failure and a successful person will help answer the question.

The successful person knows precisely what she desires, has a plan for getting it, believes in her ability to get it, and devotes a major portion of her time to acquiring it. The failure has no definite purpose in life, believes that all success is the result of "luck," and moves on her own initiative only when forced to do so.

The success is a master salesperson who has learned the art of influencing others to cooperate in a friendly spirit to carry out her plans and purposes. The failure finds fault with people. She goes out of her way to let them know about her critical attitude.

The successful person thinks before she speaks. She weighs her words carefully. And she emphasizes her likes concerning people, minimizing her dislikes or not mentioning them at all. The unsuccessful person does just the opposite. She speaks first, thinks later. Her words bring only regret and embarrassment and cost her irretrievable benefits because of the resentment they engender.

The successful person expresses opinions only after having informed herself so she can do so intelligently. The failure expresses opinions on subjects about which she has little or no knowledge.

The successful person budgets time, income and expenditures. She lives within her means. The failure squanders time and income with a contemptuous disregard for their value.

The successful person takes a keen interest in people, especially those with whom she has something in common, and cultivates a bond of friendship with them. The failure cultivates only those from whom she wants something.

The successful person is open-minded and tolerant on all subjects, toward all people. The failure has a closed mind, steeped in intolerance, which shuts her off from the recognition of favorable opportunities and the friendly cooperation of others.

The successful person keeps abreast of the times and makes it an important responsibility to know what is going on, not only in her own business, profession or community but throughout the entire world. The failure concerns herself only with her immediate needs, acquiring them by whatever means are available—fair or foul.

The successful person keeps her mind and outlook on life positive at all times. She recognizes that the space she occupies in the world and the success she enjoys depend upon the quality and quantity of service she renders. She makes it a habit to render more service than she promises. The failure looks for "something for nothing," or something under the table which she did not earn. And when she fails to get it, she blames the greed of others.

The successful person has a keen respect for her Creator and expresses it frequently through prayers and deeds of helpfulness to others. The failure believes in nothing but her own desire for food and shelter and seeks those at the expense of others when and where she can.

All in all, there is a big difference in both the words and the deeds of the successful person and the failure. But each person is where she is and what she is because of her own mental attitude toward herself and others.

Strength Grows
Out of Struggle

Struggle is a clever device through which Nature compels humanity to develop, expand and progress. It is either an ordeal or a magnificent experience, depending on one's attitude toward it. Success is impossible—unthinkable even—without it.

Life, from birth to death, is literally an unbroken chain of ever-increasing, unavoidable struggle. The education we receive from the struggles we face is cumulative—we get it a little at a time from every experience we encounter.

"Do the thing," said Emerson, "and you shall have the power."

Meet struggle and master it, says Nature, and you shall have the strength and wisdom sufficient for all your needs.

The strongest trees in the forest aren't those most protected; they are those that must struggle against the elements and other trees—and surmount them—to survive.

My grandfather was a wagon maker. In clearing his

land for crops, he always left a few oak trees standing in the open fields where they were exposed to the full force of the blazing sun and blasts of wind.

The trees that strained against Nature were far stronger and tougher than the protected oaks deep in the forest. It was timber from the trees that had struggled that he used for the wagon wheels, bending them into arc-shaped segments, without fear that they would break. Because they had struggled, they had grown strong enough to bear the heaviest loads.

Struggle similarly toughens the human spirit. Most people try to go through life following the path of least resistance. They fail to recognize that this philosophy is what makes rivers crooked—and sometimes does the same for human beings. Without the strength of character that grows out of struggle, we would be mightily tempted to flow through life with little purpose or plan.

Once we understand the broad purpose of life, we become reconciled to the circumstances that force us to struggle. As a result, we accept struggle for what it is—*opportunity*.

Struggle forces us to move when we would otherwise stand still. And it leads us eventually to the full realization that success comes only through struggle. Nothing worthwhile in life is ever achieved without a struggle. If it were easy, everyone would do it. Wherever you find a successful person, you will find a person who has struggled in his or her life. Life is a struggle and the rewards go to those who meet difficulty face to face, overcome it, and move on to the next challenge.

My first boss after I finished business college was General Rufus A. Ayers, whose law practice was so extensive that I often had to help him at night and during holidays.

At the end of each of these sessions, he always apologized for causing me to work such long hours. But he added: "You've been a big help to me—but a bigger help to yourself through the experience you've gained this evening."

And I'll never forget the answer I received when I once asked one of Henry Ford's top aides for his formula for success. "I manage to get in the way of men like Mr. Ford," he said, "and hope that when they want something done they'll call on me."

By running to embrace struggle, rather than trying to avoid it, you, too, can use it to help you learn, grow—and succeed.

Sincerity

To achieve success, you have to have a *definite goal* in life. Your chances of attaining that goal will be infinitely greater if you have a sincere wish to provide others with a better product or service. The operative word in that sentence is *sincere*.

Sincerity is a trait that pays off in self-satisfaction, self-respect and the spiritual ability to live with ourselves twenty-four hours a day. We conduct ourselves so we have the fullest respect for that invisible "other self" who can guide us to glory, fame and riches—or relegate us to misery and failure.

A friend of Abraham Lincoln once told him that his enemies were saying terrible things about him behind his back.

"I don't care what they say," exclaimed Lincoln, "so long as they're not telling the truth." Sincerity of purpose made Lincoln immune to fear of criticism.

Sincerity is a matter of motive. Therefore, it's something that others have a right to question before granting you their time, energy or money. Before embarking on a course of action, test your sincerity yourself. Ask yourself this question: "Granted I'm seeking personal gain in what I'm about to do. But am I giving fair value in service or goods for the profit or wages I hope to make, or am I hoping to get something for nothing?" Sincerity is one of the hardest things to prove to others. But you must be prepared—and eager—to do so.

Martha Berry founded a school for mountain boys and girls from a poor section of North Georgia whose parents couldn't pay for their education. Keeping the school afloat financially was difficult in the early days and she constantly needed money to carry on her work. Finally, she was able to arrange an appointment to meet with Henry Ford. She explained what she was doing and asked Ford for a modest donation. He refused.

"Well, then," said Miss Berry, "will you give us a bushel of peanuts?"

The novelty of the request so amused Ford that he gave her the money for the peanuts. Miss Berry helped her students plant and replant the peanuts until they had piled up a considerable sum of money. Then she took the money back to Ford to show how she had multiplied his small donation. Ford was so impressed that he donated enough tractors and farm equipment to put her school farm on a self-supporting basis. Through the years he gave more than one million dollars to help build the beautiful stone buildings which now stand on the campus.

"I couldn't help being impressed," he said, "with her sincerity and the marvelous way she applied it on behalf of needy boys and girls." Her belief in what she was doing was so strong that by her deeds she convinced the skeptical Ford to do what he had at first refused to do. She had demonstrated beyond all reasonable expectation that she was engaged in an endeavor so worthy that she would never succumb to adversity.

When the going gets tough—and it always does at times—your sincerity of purpose will sustain you through the difficult periods. If you know in your heart that you are providing real value for the dollar earned, your conviction will be evident to those with whom you do business.

You can achieve your own goals in life by proving to others that you have a sincere desire to help them. If you do, you won't need to worry about lean times. You will have more clients or customers than you can handle.

Hopefulness

Hope is the raw material with which you build success. It crystallizes into faith, faith into determination, and determination into action. It springs principally from your imagination, from your dreams of a better world, a better life, a better tomorrow.

On the basis of hope, you will decide upon your definite goal in life and translate it into actuality. Years ago, for example, the great railroad man James J. Hill was simply a clerk sitting at a telegraph key sending the message from a woman to a friend whose husband had been killed. He was inspired by what the message said: "Your grief can be softened by your hope of meeting your husband in a better world."

The word *hope* stuck in Hill's mind. He began thinking about the powers and possibilities of hope. That led him to dream of someday building a new railroad to the West. That dream developed into a clear-cut determination which Hill carried to fruition. The telegraph operator's dream, built on the possibilities in a single word, went on to become the Great Northern Railway system.

Hill made multimillionaires of many others along the way because he recognized that the success of his railroad was tied to the fortunes of his customers. He persuaded farmers, apple growers, miners and lumbermen to move west and transport their goods on his Great Northern Railway. Hill built an empire that eventually stretched from Canada to Missouri, and from the Great Lakes to Puget Sound. He even expanded to the Orient with his own steamship line.

Manuel L. Quezon dared to dream of and hope for self-government for his beloved Philippine Islands. He even dared hope that someday he might be president of a free Philippine republic. His hope became a deep faith which he turned into action, as he campaigned to be appointed resident commissioner of the islands.

For twenty-four years he bent every effort toward the day when the territory would become a separate country. I know, because he was my good friend and he let me advise him frequently on ways to achieve his political aims. The day he was elected president of the new Philippine republic, Quezon sent me this telegram: "May I thank you from the fullness of my heart for having inspired me to keep the fires of hope burning in my heart until this glorious day of triumph."

The lesson for you in Quezon's story is that you must give your imagination free rein to create hope. Dare to dream large dreams. Fill yourself with the faith that nothing is impossible. As Thoreau said, "If you have built castles in the air, your work need not be lost; there is where they should be. Now put foundations under them."

From your hope and faith, decide on a definite goal. Write it down. Commit it to memory. Make it the fixed star on which you chart your course to success. Then act to make it come true. When you have your eye firmly fixed on your guiding star, it is much easier to steer toward your goal. And you can quickly decide which actions will get you there quickly and which will delay you. Without your eye on the star, you may make many false turns before you finally reach your destination.

Never forget that every dream begins with hope. Every success story with a happy ending starts with the words: "Once upon a time there was a man or woman who hoped that someday . . ." Yours must start out the same way.

Patience

Americans are in a hurry. People from other countries regard this as our most singular characteristic. And they're right. It's a national trait arising from the questing, forceful energy that is our greatest source of strength.

But this same energy—this driving force that demands immediate action—can also be a source of weakness, for it has made us the most impatient people in the world. In times of war, many of our soldiers have found themselves at a fatal disadvantage due to their typically American impatience. Frequently, they exposed themselves to fire unnecessarily instead of trying to outwit a sniper.

In business, the result can be the same. We want the contracts signed and the deals done, and we want them done now. We often fail to take the time to think a project through because of our bias toward action. Because of our impatience and in our haste to "get on with it," we may give away an important advantage to others who are willing to wait a little longer before taking action. "He that can have patience," Benjamin Franklin said, "can have what he will."

Patience demands its own peculiar type of courage. It's a persistent type of forbearance and fortitude that results from complete dedication to an ideal or goal. Patience is, as Browning said, the courage to change the things you can, the willingness to accept the things you cannot and the wisdom to know the difference. Therefore, the more strongly you are imbued with the idea of achieving your principal goal in life, the more patience you will have to overcome obstacles.

The patience I'm talking about is dynamic rather than static, active rather than passive. It's a positive force to direct your destiny rather than an acquiescent submission to the circumstances or condition in which you find yourself. And it springs from the same type of immense energy that we Americans possess in such abundance. However, it is closely controlled and tightly channeled toward a single goal with almost fanatical fixation.

Knowing where you are going in life increases your tolerance for the little annoyances that come between you and your goal. You know that you are going to get there and that these are merely temporary delays. If you recognize them for what they are and approach them positively, you will find that once you are willing to face them, they will dissolve. They will disappear long before your determination does.

Constance Bannister considered impatience her greatest fault, yet she deliberately went into a profession where patience is the greatest prerequisite—photographing babies—and became one of the most successful people in the field.

"With a baby, to get the expression you want, you

must repeat and repeat, explain and explain, in a soothing monotone voice," she said. "I like photographing babies because it helps *me* so much. It develops my sense of humor and helps me to be creative in other fields."

How can you develop patience? It's easy, provided you have determined your definite goal in life and concentrate on it with all your will until you are filled with a burning desire to achieve it—and your every thought, action and prayer is directed toward that end.

It was exactly this same sort of fixed idea that provided the patience necessary for Edison to invent the electric light, for Salk to produce a polio vaccine, for Hillary to climb Mount Everest, and for Helen Keller to triumph over seemingly insurmountable physical handicaps.

The same sort of concentration on your major goal will provide the patience you need to achieve it.

Flexibility

We want to be liked. We want the approbation and friendship of others. More than that, we know that unless we can win the close, friendly cooperation of our associates, it will be difficult to achieve success in life. The number one trait of a pleasing personality is flexibility.

Flexibility means the ability to bend mentally and physically, to adapt one's self to any circumstances or environment while maintaining self-control and composure.

But flexibility does not denote pliability. You need not let yourself be subject to the whims and wills of others in order to have a flexible mentality. Few people appreciate a yes-man or -woman.

Flexibility, perhaps, can best be described as the ability to survey and assess a given situation swiftly and react to it on the basis of logic and reason with a minimum of emotion. By developing flexibility you are prepared to take prompt action in seizing opportunity or solving problems. It can help you become decisive.

Flexibility helped Arthur Nash, a Cincinnati mail-order clothier, to adjust swiftly when his business went bankrupt. He took all his employees into partnership with him on a profit-sharing-plus-wages basis and re-built the firm into one of the most profitable of its kind.

Sometimes, the flexibility of others can help you. For example, Henry Ford tended to be abrupt and short of patience with employees and business associates. Often, the flexible diplomacy of his wife, Clara, influenced him to have forbearance and saved him many difficulties.

The head of the Bank of America in San Francisco once said, "When we hire men and women, we rate them on four traits: loyalty, dependability, flexibility and ability to do a given job well."

A sense of humor is an important ingredient in flex-ibility as well. Abraham Lincoln often had to rely on his own inherent good spirits to hold his temperamental cabinet members together in moments of crisis.

Humility—as distinguished from the Uriah Heep–type of humbleness—is also necessary. How else will you ever achieve that great degree of flexibility nec-essary to voice the words *I was wrong* as everyone must do someday?

Lack of such flexibility cost President Woodrow Wil-son the Senate's approval of his cherished League of Nations project—and broke his heart. If he had throt-tled his pride and invited Senator Lodge—the League's chief opponent—to the White House for a conference, he might have won the Senate's sanction.

Flexibility is the one trait that softens poverty and adorns riches, for it helps you to be grateful for your blessings and unabashed by misfortune. It also can help you to make beneficial use of every experience of life, whether pleasant or unpleasant.

Enthusiasm

Ralph Waldo Emerson once said, "Nothing great is ever achieved without enthusiasm."

In the great Mormon Tabernacle in Salt Lake City a guest speaker was billed to speak for forty-five minutes. He spoke for more than two hours. When he finished, ten thousand men and women arose and cheered him for five minutes.

What did the speaker say to get that kind of reaction? What he said was not nearly as important as the way he said it. The crowd was swept away by the speaker's enthusiasm, and most probably didn't remember many of the details about what he said.

Louis Victor Eytinge was serving a life sentence in an Arizona state prison. He had no friends, no lawyer and no money. But he did have enthusiasm which he used so effectively that it bought him his freedom.

Eytinge wrote to the Remington Typewriter Company relating his plight and asking the company to sell him a typewriter on credit. The company did better than that. It gave him a typewriter.

He began writing business firms asking for their sales literature—which he rewrote and returned to them. His copywriting was so effective that he soon had enough money, from voluntary donations, to hire a lawyer. His work was so good, in fact, that it caught the attention of a big New York advertising agency which, with the help of his lawyer, got him pardoned. As he walked out of the prison, he was met by the agency head who greeted him with these words: "Well, Eytinge, your enthusiasm has proved more powerful than the iron bars of this prison."

The agency had a job waiting for him.

Frequent repetition has not blemished the old adage that "nothing is so catching as enthusiasm." Enthusiasm is the radio wave by which you transmit your personality to others. It is more powerful than logic, reason or rhetoric in getting your ideas across and in winning over others to your viewpoint.

A highly successful sales manager says enthusiasm is the single most important trait of a good salesman—provided it is sincere and forthright. "When you shake hands, put something extra into it that will make the other fellow feel you are genuinely happy to see him," he says.

A word of caution: Nothing is quite so phony as false enthusiasm—the excessively energetic, overwhelming display that anyone can recognize and everyone distrusts.

An example of how your own enthusiasm can carry you on to great success is afforded in the career and life of Jennings Randolph. After graduating from Salem

College in West Virginia, Randolph went into politics and waged such a forceful campaign that he was elected to Congress by a landslide over an older, more experienced opponent. Because of his success in influencing fellow representatives, President Franklin D. Roosevelt chose him to steer special wartime legislation through the House.

In a private popularity survey conducted by a group of Washington professors, Roosevelt and Randolph were voted unanimously as the most charming personalities in government service at the time—but Randolph took the lead over the President on this score through his capacity to influence others with his boundless enthusiasm. After fourteen years in Congress, Randolph decided to accept one of the many offers he received from private industry.

He became assistant to the president of Capital Airlines while the company was operating in the red. Within two years, he had helped, with his matchless energy, to raise the company above all other airlines in earnings.

Speaking of Randolph's pleasing personality, the president of Capital Airlines said about Randolph: "He more than earns his salary, not alone by the actual work he performs—but more especially for the enthusiasm he inspires among other members of the firm."

No one is born enthusiastic; it is an acquired trait. You can acquire it also. Remember that in almost every contact with others, you are trying, in a sense, to sell them something. That's true in all but trivial relationships. First convince yourself of the value of your idea, your product, your service—or yourself. Examine it—or yourself—critically. Learn the flaws in whatever you are trying to sell and immediately correct them. Be thoroughly convinced of the *rightness* of your product or idea.

Armed with this conviction, cultivate the habit of thinking positively, forcefully and energetically, and you will find enthusiasm developing in and of itself— with the authoritative ring of true sincerity helping you to project it to others.

Use Your
Personal Magnetism

If you are like most people, you have met individuals to whom you are drawn irresistibly on initial contact—people you accept immediately as friends and trust far more than the average casual acquaintance. All of us possess such personal magnetism to some degree, some more than others.

Personal magnetism seems to be a biological inheritance that determines the amount of emotional feeling—such as enthusiasm, love and joy—that we are capable of generating and applying in our words and deeds. We can't increase the quality or quantity of this inheritance, but we can organize it and direct it to help us attain any desired aim. And those of us who learn to do so often become the leaders, the builders, the doers and the pioneers who help to advance our civilization.

While this is often the case, it is not the rule. It frequently happens that unworthy persons possess this great power to influence others. Therefore, it behooves us to apply an extra measure of caution when dealing with such people until certain of their intentions and motives. The important thing, however, is that you can put your personal magnetism to work for you to achieve success. With it, you can obtain the friendly cooperation of others to help you attain your principal goals.

Personal magnetism is revealed mainly through the voice, eyes and hands—the principal means we have of communicating with others. But your very bearing and posture play a significant part in it too. The actual words used may be quite meaningless, but the tone of voice and force of delivery and enthusiasm with which they are given may be far more powerful than the logic and rhetoric they offer.

For that matter, a person possessing an extremely high degree of personal magnetism may not have to speak a word to draw people to his side. An outstanding example is the Reverend Billy Graham. He draws souls to the Creator by a mere gesture, with a glance from his expressive eyes or through a melodiously voiced phrase. Franklin Roosevelt had this same power over others in the political arena. But, I must point out, so did Hitler, Mussolini and many other unsavory characters throughout history. Beware of those who seek to use their personal magnetism for destructive ends.

You can put this same power to work for you if you learn to exude self-confidence, spiritual strength and authority. Make a conscious effort to meet the gaze of others more directly, to clasp their hands firmly and warmly, to speak in pleasant, forthright tones with volume pitched and timbre gauged to capture the interest of your listeners.

Turn on your personal magnetism—see what it can do for you!

Have Confidence
in Yourself

When Thomas Edison believed he had discovered the means by which a machine records and reproduces the sound of the human voice, he called in a model maker, gave him a rough pencil drawing of his idea and asked that a working model be built.

The model maker looked at the drawing for a moment, then exclaimed, "Impossible! You'll never make that thing work."

"What makes you think it won't work?" Edison asked.

"Because no one has ever made a machine that could talk," exclaimed the model maker.

Edison could have accepted the verdict and given up his idea of a talking machine. But his mind didn't work that way.

"Go ahead and build the model just like this drawing," Edison demanded, "and let me be the loser if it doesn't work."

The person who backs his ideas and plans with self-confidence always has the advantage over those who give up and quit at the first signs of defeat.

The model was completed, and to the great surprise of the model maker, it worked on the first test.

Success doesn't crown the person who sells himself short through lack of self-confidence. It does favor the person who knows what he wants, is determined to get it and refuses to accept the word *impossible*.

One of the most successful insurance sales managers in America requires all of his salespeople to spend five minutes before a mirror every morning before starting work looking at themselves and saying, "You are the greatest living salesperson and you are going to prove it today, tomorrow and always." And by prearrangement with the sales manager, the spouses of each of these salespeople see them off to work at the door each morning with this message, "You are the greatest salesperson living and you will prove it today."

It is significant that these salespeople are leading all others in a field—insurance—that is said to be something which must be sold, but is never voluntarily bought.

The subconscious section of the human mind has unlimited powers that each individual may tap and direct to any desired end. Yet the method by which one may direct it is so simple that many people discount its workability. Briefly stated, the subconscious can be directed by simply talking to it and giving it orders as if it were an invisible person standing ready with the power and the willingness to do whatever is requested of it.

The subconscious has one very peculiar trait. It believes everything everyone tells it, and acts accordingly. It not only believes and acts upon one's spoken words, but more astounding still, it believes in and acts upon one's thoughts—especially those thoughts which are highly emotionalized with either faith or fear.

The subconscious is also very amenable to the repetition of thoughts and words. This trait is fortunate because it is the simple means by which one can put the subconscious to work on one's behalf for any desired purpose. It also explains why the person who allows his mind to dwell upon poverty and failure and ill health, and all the things he does not want, is plagued by getting just those things.

Every successful person has a system for conditioning his mind to feed the subconscious with aims and purposes of his own choice, and to do it so intensely that it has no opportunity to attract anything that is not desired. The technique of the system is unimportant as long as it conveys to the subconscious, by repetition, a clear description of what is wanted.

Use your subconscious to build your self-confidence, and you will train your mind to serve you in everything you do.

Strengthen Your Sense of Humor

A sense of humor can smooth the bumps on the road of success. If you are one of those people who is blessed with a cheerful disposition, count yourself fortunate. If not, you can develop one.

It's obvious that a good sense of humor makes you a more likable, more attractive person. That alone will help you achieve success. But more than that, it can help you overcome momentary failures, to rise above them and seek out new courses of action that will put you back on the success track.

A keen sense of humor is based chiefly on humility. It was this type of constant good humor that permitted Minnie Lee Steen and her four small children to endure severe hardships in the Utah deserts while her husband, Charles, hunted for uranium.

Through two long and arduous years, Charles and Minnie Lee Steen kept their sense of humor. For the children, they made a game of their troubles—a game of "pioneer" they enjoyed hugely. As a result, their troubles never had a chance to crush the plucky family.

In the end, Steen won. He struck uranium on a claim that in three years produced seventy million dollars worth of ore and was eventually worth millions more. Charles and Minnie Lee Steen moved from the pit of poverty to the top of the world.

What the Steens and thousands of others have done, you can also do. First of all, learn to count your blessings and assets more often than you do your troubles and problems, and put them uppermost in your mind. If you have difficulty doing this, make a written inventory of them and read them over to yourself whenever you start worrying. Remember, many of your blessings are hidden treasures, commonplace everyday items or qualities that you simply take for granted. Your health, for example or the love, admiration and faith your family has for you.

Learn to regard your problems as stepping-stones to success. Each one you overcome brings you closer to your goal. Remember that every bad situation could be worse—like the man who cursed his luck because he had no shoes, until he met a man who had no feet. Never let a day go by without a prayer of thanks for the bounty you enjoy, no matter how small it is. And go out of your way every day to spend part of your time and energy helping others.

Remember, too, that no problem is unique or new. You can always seek advice or help from others who have been there. And you are never alone. A greater power is with you always. Make it a policy to meet your problems head-on, in a spirit of audacity, courage and decisiveness. As Emerson said, "An adventure is nothing more than an inconvenience, rightly considered."

Showmanship

Consider the case of Joe Dull. Joe's a hardworking guy, diligent, faithful, punctual, dependable and resourceful. He gives his company more than it's due in time, effort and energy. It would seem that Joe is bound to achieve success.

But he won't. Joe isn't going anywhere. Others, considerably less worthy, are getting the promotions and raises. The fact is that Joe lacks showmanship. He simply never attracts the attention of the right people.

Are you like Joe? If so, develop showmanship and watch how much easier it is to climb the ladder of success. However, before you say, "Eureka, that's it. There's my answer," remember this cautionary note. There is a distinct difference between true showmanship and less honest ways of attracting attention to yourself. Apple-polishing, for example, will gain you more enemies than friends. So will outright boastfulness. True showmanship is creative. It has, as the name implies, a certain entertainment value. It demands ingenuity and a good sense of timing.

Bernard MacFadden's flair for showmanship, for example, sometimes bordered on the bizarre. But he made it pay off in millions by parachuting in red flannel underwear from airplanes and by walking down Broadway in his bare feet to create enormous publicity for all his enterprises.

You needn't go to such extremes. Sometimes special attention to the niceties of courtesy and politeness can achieve the same proposes.

Glenn R. Fouche, former president of the Stayform Company, tells the story of a friend who rose to become president of a large hoist-and-derrick company in Texas by using showmanship.

A young salesman, when he sold his first small hoist, he wrote the head of the shipping department thanking him for getting the order delivered promptly. He wrote the paint department to tell how proud he was when he saw the bright red finish as the hoist was unpacked. Through the years, he made a point of trying to let each member of the firm know how worthwhile he thought their services were.

By appreciating the value of others, he became the most appreciated man in the firm!

Remember that true showmanship must follow a positive course. It never knocks or minimizes the value of other people. No one can climb to success on someone else's shoulders. Also, if you are like good old dependable Joe Dull, you may be too modest or too shy and retiring to present your ideas to the right people in person. If that's the case, write memos. Putting an idea in writing ensures that credit goes where credit is due.

But don't wait. Start now to use showmanship as a tool to build your success!

Choose Your Goal

You wouldn't think of beginning a long automobile trip without knowing where you were going and having a map to guide you.

But only about two people in every hundred know precisely what they desire from life and have workable plans for attaining their goals. These are the men and women who are the leaders in every walk of life—the big successes who have made life pay off on their terms.

The strangest thing about these people is that they have no more opportunities than others who have never made the grade.

If you know exactly what you want and have absolute faith in your ability to get it, you can achieve success. If you are not sure what you want from life, start now, this very minute, and decide definitely what you want, how much of it you want and when you want to have it in your possession.

There is a precise four-point formula for achieving your goals:

1. Write out a clear statement of what you desire most—the one thing or circumstance which, after you attain it, would in your opinion make you successful.
2. Write out a clear outline of the plan by which you intend to attain this objective and clearly state what you intend to give in return.
3. Set a definite time limit within which you intend to acquire the object of your definite purpose.
4. Memorize what you have written and repeat it many times daily as a prayer. End the prayer by expressing gratitude for having received that for which your plan calls.

Follow these instructions carefully and you may be amazed at how soon your entire life will change for the better. This formula will lead you into an alliance with an invisible partner who will remove obstacles from your path and attract to you favorable opportunities of which you may never have dreamed. Keep this procedure to yourself so you will not be disturbed by skeptics who may not understand the profound law you are following.

Remember, nothing ever "just happens." Someone has to make things happen, including individual successes. Success in every calling is the result of definite action, carefully planned and persistently carried out by the person who conditions his mind for success and believes he will attain it.

Walter P. Chrysler spent his life savings to purchase a car because he intended to go into automobile manufacturing and he needed to know all about them. He tore the car apart and reassembled it scores of times to the amazement of his friends, who began to think he was mentally unbalanced. Nevertheless, he stood fast by his purpose and went on to become one of the great industrial successes of his time.

Chrysler's story should give you hope, for you must realize that little education and lack of working capital need not discourage you from choosing any goal you desire in life.

Marie Curie revealed the existence of radium before anyone else had done so. And Dr. Albert Einstein led the way to the splitting of the atom and the resultant release of power, which other people with less definiteness of purpose than he believed was impossible.

Definiteness of purpose makes the word *impossible* obsolete. It is the starting point of all success. It is available to you and everyone—without money and without price. All you need is personal intiative to embrace it and use it.

Unless you know what you want from life and are determined to get it, you will be forced to accept the mere crumbs left by others who knew where they were going and had a plan for getting there.

To be sure of success, saturate your mind completely with your goal. Think and plan about that which you desire. Keep your mind off that which you do not want. You have here the practical formula which all successful people follow.

Use Your Personal Initiative

It would be difficult to name a more destructive human habit than procrastination—putting off until tomorrow what should have been done last week. Personal initiative is the only cure for procrastination. Successful people are those who think and move on their personal initiative. There are two forms of action, that in which one engages from choice, and that in which one indulges only when forced to do so.

We live in a country that abounds in privilege and personal freedoms available to rich and poor alike. It is perhaps the most important factor in our system of free enterprise.

The privilege of personal initiative was considered of such great importance that it is specifically guaranteed to every citizen in the Constitution of the United States. And it is of such great value that every well-managed business recognizes and properly rewards individuals who use their personal initiative to better the company.

When Andrew Carnegie was a young clerk in the office of the division superintendent of the Pennsylvania

Railroad Company in Pittsburgh, he came to the office one morning and discovered that there had been a bad train wreck just outside the city. He tried desperately to reach the superintendent by telephone but was unable to do so.

Finally, in desperation, he did something which he knew could mean his automatic discharge because of the company's strict rules. Recognizing that every minute of delay was costing the railroad a fortune, he wired instructions to the conductor, signing the boss's name.

When the superintendent came to his desk several hours later, he found Carnegie's resignation and an explanation of what he had done. The day passed and nothing happened. The next day Carnegie's resignation was sent back to him with these words written in red ink across the face of the letter: RESIGNATION REFUSED.

Several days later, his boss called Carnegie into his office and said, "Young man, there are two kinds of people who never get ahead or amount to anything. One is the fellow who will not do what he is told, and the other is the fellow who will not do anything more than he is told." In this instance, the boss found Carnegie more valuable than the railroad's policies.

Several years ago, George Stefek of Chicago was convalescing at a veterans hospital. As he lay there he got an idea, a simple one that anyone could have conceived. But the important thing was that Stefek acted upon it as soon as he got out of the hospital. It paid off handsomely for him.

What Stefek did was find a use for the blank pieces of cardboard laundries used to stiffen shirts they had laundered. Stefek sold advertising space on the cardboards. As a result, he could sell the cardboards to the laundries thirty percent cheaper and provided advertisers a new medium to reach prospects. George Stefek built American Shirtboard Advertising Company into a thriving business.

Clarence Saunders of Memphis, Tennessee, saw a long line of people waiting to serve themselves in what was then a new type of restaurant—a cafeteria. He put his imagination to work and came up with a plan to adapt the self-service idea to the grocery business.

When he explained his idea to his employer, a local grocer, he was told that he was paid to pack and deliver groceries, and that he should not waste his time on foolish, impractical ideas. Saunders quit his job and carried out his plan under the name of Piggly Wiggly Stores. He made millions from his idea, the forerunner of today's modern supermarkets.

By giving us absolute control over our power to think, the Creator no doubt intended that we should use that prerogative through our own initiative.

The overworked alibi of the procrastinator—"I haven't had time"—has probably caused more failures than all other alibis combined. The people who get ahead and make a place for themselves *always find time* to move on their own initiative in any direction necessary for their advancement or benefit.

Get the Job
You Want

The service you perform in your daily work is a commodity that you must try to market to the best advantage. Notice, please, that I did not write "at the highest possible price." The best job offered you may not always be the one with the highest pay. Other jobs may offer greater chances for advancement, more opportunity to learn, to gain experience and to prepare yourself for higher positions.

Always take the long-range view in job hunting. Look for opportunity rather than a mere immediate subsistence. Here's the way one man went hunting for opportunity rather than waiting for it to knock on his door:

When he graduated from an eastern engineering college, John Wesley Ashton decided to market his services with the same skill a businessman puts into marketing his products. First he decided what kind of position he wanted and the amount of salary he desired. Then he inserted the following advertisement in all the daily newspapers he could afford:

"Mr. Top Executive in the engineering field: Are you willing to let a graduate engineer demonstrate what he can be worth to you by working for one month without pay? I can bring you loyalty, dependability, patience, ability to get along with others harmoniously, a powerhouse of enthusiasm, a pleasing personality, punctuality and an enduring passion to learn as I earn, as well as a scholastic record as a summa cum laude graduate in engineering."

The advertisement drew more than three hundred replies! An executive of U.S. Steel wrote: "Meet me at our headquarters in New York next Wednesday and, if you are as good as you say, you may as well bring your baggage and be prepared to go with me to one of our plants."

Ashton's approach was so unique, it was certain to attract attention. The offer to work a month without pay was a challenge to business executives. It proved he was more interested in demonstrating what he had to give than in what he hoped to get out of the job. And the personal traits he listed, instead of sounding boastful, told the prospective employer what he hoped to prove about himself in the month of gratis work.

At his interview with the steel executive, Ashton handed over a neatly typed leather-bound brochure telling everything about himself—education, civic and charitable affiliations, hobbies, news items about himself from the college paper and personal data. It also included a recent photograph and a list of references.

Ashton got the job and he didn't have to work the month without pay. It was agreed that his salary would be fixed by mutual agreement at the end of the first month after he had demonstrated his ability. Even so, John Wesley Ashton took the job at less than he was offered by another employer, because he recognized that the post had almost unlimited opportunities for promotion.

This account of Ashton's approach should stimulate your ingenuity in applying for work in any field of endeavor. Use your imagination. Ask yourself these questions: How can I attract a busy executive's attention? How can I offer to demonstrate the value of my services?

Be sure not to oversell yourself. Don't promise something you can't deliver. Exaggeration is at best a shaky foundation on which to build a career. Instead, let the boss be pleasantly surprised to discover that you are giving him even more than you said you would—it may even push you another rung up the ladder.

Get a Promotion

So you think you're in a rut. It's been a long time since you got a raise or a promotion. What can you do about it? For starters, let's look at it from the boss's point of view.

Human nature is the same whether a person is the employer or the employee. The same things that motivate you motivate bosses. They want to succeed, to increase their businesses, to increase their personal incomes. Otherwise they would be off playing golf rather than risking their capital and expending their energies at their desks.

Your employer wants to promote you and give you raises—if you make it worth her while. If you help her achieve her goals, she is bound to help you achieve yours. If she doesn't, she is not the type of person you should be working for.

The surest way to success is to render more and better service than is expected of you. If you just barely fulfill your daily quota, if you perform only what is required, if you show no interest in the firm's welfare—you have no right to expect advancement.

Perhaps it's time to jar yourself out of your lethargy and wage a definite campaign to get out of that rut. Start with the philosophy that the boss isn't going to promote you—you are going to promote yourself.

Begin by seizing every opportunity to demonstrate your ability to hold a higher position. Instead of shirking responsibility, go out of your way to seek it. When others pass the buck, you be the one to make decisions. *The most significant mark of leadership is the willingness to make decisions and accept responsibility for them.*

Decide on the job you want and train yourself for it. Take advantage of company training programs or attend adult-education courses offered by your local school or college. Or tell the boss frankly that you want to learn how to fill that job and you would appreciate her help.

Above all, keep the boss's viewpoint in mind. Remember, if you have been successful in your effort, you will probably be a boss yourself someday. Take the same interest in the firm that your boss does. Try to see the plant, the office or the shop through her eyes.

In adopting this attitude, you'll condition your mind toward an executive outlook. You will find yourself thinking of increased production, lower costs, bigger sales and larger profits. You'll find yourself bubbling with ideas to achieve those aims.

Let your enthusiasm and imagination roam. Don't be afraid of an idea because it's novel or daring. And don't let negative-minded people deter you with the argument, "It's never been tried before." That's all the more reason for trying it.

Start with the job you now hold. How can it be performed faster, better, more efficiently, cheaper? What operations can be eliminated or merged? What changes would result in a superior product at less cost?

Almost every company these days has a suggestion system to take advantage of the brainpower offered by its employees. Through it, you can present your ideas to the boss. If your firm lacks such a system, a simple note will do.

Remember, however, your efforts for promotion must be sincere. No one is quite as phony as the apple-polisher and the yes-man. You can test yourself on this point. If you are sincerely trying to help the company, you will enjoy a keen sense of personal satisfaction, whether or not you receive immediate recognition from your superior.

Make sure your ideas are positive. You can't climb to success by pushing others down. If your ideas consist of complaining about or criticizing your fellow workers—forget it. Your ideas should be of the type that will create new jobs and higher income for everyone.

Remember, too, that no ideas are worth noting without a plan of action. If you consider an idea worthwhile, do something about it—immediately. Try it out yourself if you're in a position to do so, or take it to the person who can. But don't let it die untried.

Without action, an idea is never born. And nothing is more tragic than the stillbirth of a good idea.

How One Man
Won a Promotion

Carol Downes gave up his job as a bank teller and took a position with W. C. Durant, who had just recently formed the automobile company that eventually became General Motors. After six months on the job, Downes decided it was time to see what the chances were for a promotion. He went to Durant with a questionnaire that asked how Downes could improve his services to the company, what were his greatest faults and virtues in his work and finally, "What position higher than my present one am I qualified to hold?"

Durant was amused with the sheer brass demonstrated by Downes' questionnaire. He gave it back to him with only the last question answered. He had written, "You are hereby appointed to supervise the installation of machinery and equipment in our new assembly plant, with no promise of either promotion or increased pay."

Durant also gave Downes a series of blueprints, showing where the machinery was to be installed and said, "Here are the instructions for you to follow. Now let's see what you can do with them."

Downes took the blueprints and quickly discovered that with no engineering training, he couldn't even read them. It was here that he demonstrated his qualities of leadership. Instead of admitting that he'd bitten off more than he could chew, he went out and found the right man to do the job. That is the essence of leadership.

Downes hired an engineering firm to supervise installation of the machinery under his direction and paid the fee from his own pocket. As he walked to Durant's office to report that the job had been completed—a week ahead of schedule—he passed a row of executive offices. One gave him quite a shock; it was lettered CAROL DOWNES, GENERAL MANAGER.

Durant told him he was being promoted to that position with enough zeros in his salary to make it worthwhile.

"When I gave you those blueprints, I knew you couldn't read them," Durant said. "But I wanted to see how you would handle the situation. Your resourcefulness in finding someone to do the job marked you as good executive material. If you had come back with an alibi instead of a complete job, I would have fired you."

Downes went on to become a multimillionaire. When I last met him, he was in "retirement" but was actually serving as advisor to the Southern Governors' Association as a dollar-a-year man—still going the extra mile and having a lot of fun doing it.

Lend a Helping Hand

Everyone who reaches the top receives substantial boosts along the way from others. The simple law of fair play requires that we respond by helping others.

The turning point in my own career, for example, came when Andrew Carnegie advised me to begin organizing the "Science of Success" as a definitive philosophy of knowledge, and gave me his active help and support to do so. I hope that in passing on what I learned in a lifetime of research, I am paying off the debt incurred when Carnegie lent me his aid so many decades ago.

It is a fact that one of the surest ways to achieve your own success in life is by helping others to attain theirs. And almost anyone can contribute to those less fortunate. The truly affluent person is the one who can afford to give of himself, of his time and energy, to the benefit of others. In so doing, he enriches himself beyond measure.

One of the richest experiences you'll ever enjoy is to

be able to point to someone at the peak of success and say, "I helped put her there."

Your efforts on behalf of someone less fortunate not only will help him, but will also add something of priceless value to your own soul—whether or not he recognizes your aid or is grateful for it.

It is a strange fact that human nature seeks struggle, either on behalf of ourselves or others. I remember how, when I was considerably younger, I finally fought free from debt. All my obligations were discharged. I was contented—or so I thought. But as the months passed, unrest set in. It took me some time to realize what was wrong. It was the fun of the fight that I missed.

That didn't mean I had to give up my own fortune and start from scratch again. I found I could get just as much fun out of helping others fight their battles, by assuming some of their responsibilities, by making the way to success easier for them.

Think how the world would be transformed if each of us adopted someone else to help through life. In turn, each of us would be adopted and receive help.

Helping others makes good business sense. John Wanamaker, the Philadelphia merchant king, once said that the most profitable habit was that of "rendering useful service where it is not expected."

Perhaps some down-to-earth examples will help you think of ways to help others:

There is a merchant in an eastern city who has built up a successful business through a very simple process. His clerks frequently check the parking meters near the store. Wherever a clerk spots an "expired" sign, he drops a coin in the slot and attaches a note that the merchant has been happy to protect the driver against the inconvenience of a parking ticket. Many motorists drop in to thank the merchant—and stay to buy.

The owner of a big Boston men's store inserts a neatly printed card in the pocket of each suit he sells. It tells the purchaser that if he finds the suit satisfactory, he may bring the card back after six months and exchange it for a necktie. Naturally, the buyer always comes back pleased with the suit—and is a good prospect for another sale.

Another example is Butler Stork who gave of himself so freely as a prisoner in the Ohio State Penitentiary that he was released and thereby saved himself a twenty-year sentence. Stork organized a correspondence school that taught more than 1,000 inmates a variety of courses without charge to them or the state. He even induced the International Correspondence School to donate textbooks. The plan attracted so much attention that Stork was given his freedom as a reward.

Put your own mind to work. Assess your own ability and energy. Who needs your help? How can you help them? It doesn't take money. All it takes is ingenuity and a strong desire to be of genuine service.

Helping others solve their problems will help you solve your own.

Live Harmoniously
with Others

Anyone who aspires to success in life must recognize the causes of failure. How else can we avoid the pitfalls? In my research into human relations, I have found at least thirty major causes of failure. The granddaddy of them all is the *lack of ability to get along harmoniously with others.*

A great businessman—one of the wealthiest men of his day—once told me that he had a five-point measuring stick he used in choosing people for advancement to high executive jobs. The five points are:

1. Faculty for getting along with others
2. Loyalty to those to whom loyalty is due
3. Dependability under all circumstances
4. Patience in all situations
5. Ability to do a given job well.

It is notable that job ability came last. That's because the more ability one has for a task, the more objectionable one may be if lacking the other four traits.

* * *

Charles M. Schwab was promoted by Andrew Carnegie from a day laborer to a $75,000-a-year job which was a fortune in those days. But Schwab also got a bonus that sometimes reached one million dollars a year. Carnegie said the salary was for the actual service Schwab rendered. The bonus was for what he inspired others to do.

Your ability to inspire others is a blank check on the bank of life that you can fill in for whatever you desire. If you lack this ability, you can take steps to acquire it. Here are some rules to adopt and follow:

- Go out of your way to speak a kind word or render some useful service where it is not expected.
- Modify your voice to convey a feeling of warmth and friendship to those you address.
- Direct your conversation to subjects of greatest interest to your listeners. Talk "with" them rather than "to" them. Consider the persons with whom you're conversing as the most interesting in the world, at least at that moment.
- Soften your expression frequently with a smile as you speak.
- Never, under any circumstances, use profanity or obscenity.
- Keep your religious and political views to yourself.
- Never ask a favor of anyone you haven't yourself helped at some time.
- Be a good listener. Inspire others to speak freely.
- Remember that an ounce of optimism is worth a ton of pessimism.

- Close each day with this prayer: "I ask not more blessings, but more wisdom with which to make better use of the blessings I now possess. And give me, please, more understanding that I may occupy more space in the hearts of my fellow humans by rendering more service tomorrow than I have rendered today."

Let Others Help You Achieve Success

Success will come more quickly and surely if you learn how to make use of the education, experience, ability and influence of others.

Captain Eddie Rickenbacker believed his greatest personal asset was his "ability to get other people to lend me the use of their brains in a friendly spirit of cooperation.

"If I exchange the dollar I have for the dollar you have, we both end up no better off than when we started. But if I exchange an idea for the idea you have, then we both end up twice as rich as we were. And teamwork is the means of multiplying our spiritual wealth to infinity."

Remember that two or more people, working closely in an alliance in which they complement and support each other's abilities, can always achieve more than one person alone. The greatest achievements of our free-enterprise system come from group rather than individual enterprises. But in seeking the help of others, you must be prepared to make an even trade. You can't come empty-handed.

Thomas Edison's greatness as an inventor resulted from his genius for organizing teams of individuals, each with far more knowledge in his own specialty than he possessed, for a common goal.

Lloyd Weeks of Salem, Illinois, is a mechanical engineer who conceived a unique idea for constructing oil tanks. But the idea needed money to put it into development. A neighbor, who was a successful dentist, didn't have Weeks' engineering know-how, but he had some money he had saved from his dental practice. Each contributed his resources into a business alliance that has netted each of them thousands of dollars in profits month after month.

It is absolutely essential that all members of an alliance share in its benefits. Otherwise, the team will soon fall apart.

One evening, Henry Ford was walking through his plant and stopped to talk to a floor sweeper.

"Like your job?" Ford asked.

"Yep," the janitor said, "but I'd like it better if you sold these metal filings, instead of throwing them away, and gave me part of the money."

Ford put the idea into operation the next day. It saved the company a significant sum and earned a promotion for the janitor.

What do you need to achieve success? Who has it? What can you offer in return? Maybe it's exactly what someone else is seeking.

If so, you can pool your resources and make the fight for success much easier. As the old saying goes, "Ain't none of us as smart as all of us."

Welcome Help from Others

Clear thinking never comes from a worried mind. Smart people know this, and they do something about it by seeking the aid of others whose minds are not clouded by fears and worries.

During the early stages of the Great Depression, John Collier came to my office with a problem that had worried him until he was physically ill. He had the answer to his problem, but his state of mind didn't permit him to recognize it.

Mr. Collier was a shoe manufacturer in Boston. When the Depression started, the bank holding some of his notes closed him out and took over his equipment. He couldn't get another loan without collateral.

A few simple questions revealed these facts: He was an experienced shoe manufacturer of more than twenty successful years; he had an established line of buyers who had patronized him from the beginning of his business; he was a deacon in one of the most prominent churches in Boston; and his home life was happy. As I summed up his assets, I told Mr. Collier that he was rich in life's values, which count for most.

"Yes, I know," he replied, "but I'm broke!"

"A man who has the sort of assets that you possess is never broke," I replied, "because they are the best security anyone can have."

"But banks don't think so."

"No, banks don't," I explained, "but there are other ways of finding people who do. Now here is what I suggest you do: Call a meeting of ten of the most prominent men you know, men who have substantial financial means, and the same number of merchants who have been buying shoes from you. Ask them to lend you the money you need to set yourself up in business again."

I had hardly finished speaking when Mr. Collier's eyes lost the glassy look of fear. He began to smile, took a notebook from his pocket and began to write. After he finished he handed the book to me and it contained the names of only five men, each a former customer of his.

"There," he said, "are the names of the five men who will come to my rescue. They've bought shoes from me for many years; they know my product and they have confidence in both me and my shoes. I'll get the financial help I need from them by giving them an extra discount on all the shoes they buy from me in the future."

Then I explained to Mr. Collier that he had adopted the same plan which served Henry Ford so well during the early days of the Ford Motor Company. He got the operating capital he needed, I explained, from the men who purchased his automobiles—his dealers.

"It is all very clear to me now," Mr. Collier re-marked. "But what puzzles me is why I didn't think of this before coming to see you." That same question has bothered many other people who have the answers to their own problems but have to get others to reveal it to them.

Mr. Collier went back to Boston. Seven months later I received a letter from him explaining what had happened with his plan. With the letter was a fine pocket watch inscribed: "To Napoleon Hill, who introduced me to my other self."

The inscription told the entire story. All I did was to loosen Mr. Collier from the grip of fear that had caused him to set up unnecessary limitations for himself in a time of need.

The finest lesson anyone can learn is through the discovery of this fact: Our greatest asset is our ability to procure the help of those who can and will happily give us counsel when our own resourcefulness fails.

Work with Your Team

Cooperation is indispensable in your home, your job and in your social life. It is an absolute necessity in our democratic form of government and our system of free enterprise.

There are two kinds of cooperation. One is motivated by fear or need, the other is based upon voluntary willingness. Real teamwork can only be acquired by establishing the proper motive to induce friendly coordination of effort.

In the decades that have passed since Andrew Carnegie was a captain of American industry, no one has really improved his formula for inspiring teamwork. His system was simple. First he established a monetary incentive through promotions and bonuses designed so that a part of every individual's job depended on the sort of service he or she rendered. Second, he never reprimanded any employee openly, but he caused employees to reprimand themselves by asking carefully directed questions. Third, he never made decisions for his executives. He encouraged them to make their own decisions and be responsible for the results.

Carnegie's method encouraged individual achievement in a team structure because he believed that the greatest success is attained only through teamwork. This means *giving* cooperation as well as *receiving* it. Selfish leaders will get little cooperation from their subordinates because cooperation is like love in that one must give it in order to receive it.

Captain Eddie Rickenbacker inspired teamwork during two world wars in his service in the Air Force. During World War I, he personally shot down twenty-six enemy planes. And in World War II, his personal example forged a group of airmen into a team that brought them safely through the ordeal of being adrift in an open raft in the Pacific Ocean for almost a month. His brand of teamwork was also the foundation upon which he built Eastern Airlines.

Philosopher William James once said, "If you can influence others to cooperate with you in a friendly spirit, you can get anything you want with little or no resistance." That's a pretty bold statement, but it happens to be true.

When you get to the heart of any large, successful corporation, you find that its every heartbeat is teamwork, inspired from the top down. Whenever you find a winning sports team, the credit goes not to any one person, unless of course it is the coach who inspires his players to subordinate personal glory to the success of the team. Knute Rockne of Notre Dame became a legend in his lifetime for his wonderful ability to inspire teamwork.

Any adequate interpretation of the motives that induce friendly teamwork must call attention to the Sermon on the Mount. There is no better way of getting friendly cooperation than by application of the Golden Rule.

The law of reciprocation also has a negative aspect —the law of retaliation. They are both deeply seated in the nature of man. Through them, the meaning of the Biblical passage, "Whatsoever a man soweth that shall he also reap," becomes crystal clear. For it is true that whatever you do to or for another, you do to or for yourself.

Work well with your team—and your team will carry you to success.

Humility

Many people think of humility, one of the principal ingredients of a pleasing personality, as a negative virtue. But it isn't. It's a powerfully positive one. Humility is a force that you can put into operation for your own good. All of humanity's greatest advances—spiritual, cultural or material—have been based on it.

It is the prime requisite of true Judeo-Christian philosophy/theology. Also with humility, Gandhi set India free. And with its help, Dr. Albert Schweitzer helped to create a better world for Africans.

Humility is absolutely essential to the type of personality you need to achieve personal success, no matter what your goal. And you will find it even more essential after you have reached the top. Without humility, you will never gain wisdom, for one of the most important traits of a wise person is the ability to say, "I was wrong."

Without humility, you will never be able to find what I call the "seed of an equivalent benefit" in adversity and defeat. Every setback carries something with it to help you overcome it—and even to rise above it. For example, R. G. LeTourneau started in business as a garage operator, failed at that, and went into the contracting business. He was a subcontractor on the Hoover Dam project when he ran into an unexpected strata of hard stone. The difficulties and delays in removing the stubborn rock cost him everything he had.

LeTourneau didn't blame others or complain about fate treating him poorly, nor did he blame the forces of nature for his losses. He took responsibility himself. After each setback, he found comfort in prayer. It was while praying for guidance that he found the "seed of an equivalent benefit" from his last defeat. He decided to go into the business of manufacturing machines that could move any kind of rock or earth.

As a result, LeTourneau earth-moving machinery is now in use throughout the world. LeTourneau has several manufacturing plants and he amassed a personal fortune that ran into the millions. But the story of his humility doesn't stop there. To express his gratitude for the help he received in turning defeat into victory, LeTourneau made it a practice of giving most of his income to churches, and devoted most of his own time to lay preaching.

Sometimes, humility turns defeats into a spiritual blessing. Many years ago, I visited Lee Braxton, a businessman and former mayor of Whiteville, North Carolina, on the very day he discovered he had suffered a heavy financial loss due to the negligence of a business associate whom he had trusted implicitly for years.

"How many successful businesses have you built and managed?" I asked.

"About fifteen in all," Braxton said, "including the

First National Bank of Whiteville. And I never lost a penny on any of them. That's why this hurts so much. It is such an ugly jab at my pride."

"That's good," I told him. "You are about to learn that you have as much strength in times of failure as in times of success. Your loss has been a great blessing if it leaves you gifted with humility of the heart and gratitude for those riches you still possess. With it, you can be more successful than ever," I told him.

Braxton's face lit up with a broad smile. "That's right," he said. "I hadn't thought of it that way."

A few months later, I received a letter from Braxton. He said his income had climbed to an all-time high, more than making up the loss he had suffered. Humility is a positive force that knows no limitations.

Sell to Yourself

What you say and how you say it are extremely important. Others judge us by the way we speak, our vocabulary, and how we deliver our ideas and thoughts. But how we appear, not what we say, often has an equal or greater impression on others—and on ourselves. How others perceive us and how we see ourselves are both very important if we are to achieve the level of success we desire.

One of the most successful salesmen in America drives around with an expensive set of golf clubs in the trunk of his car. He has never shot a stroke of golf in his life, but you would be surprised how effectively he uses those clubs to knock down any obstacles that get in his way of making a sale.

Without ever saying so, he gives the impression of being so successful that he can spend considerable time playing golf. When he is invited to play a game, he always pleads previous appointments with the "Vandermorgans or Rockerbilts," but he never allows himself to be cornered for a game. If he ever did, he would be sunk.

Fraud? Deceit? Misrepresentation? No! He is the most successful salesman in his field. To sell successfully, he has to bolster his own ego, which harms no one. And he sells!

Personally, I've never felt the acute necessity of bolstering my ego by such things, and you probably haven't either. But if I did feel that way, I would go to any extreme required to do the job properly. Perhaps I might even go that salesman one better.

I've discovered, in dealing with thousands of men and women in every conceivable walk of life, that the human ego is a very tricky thing and has to be influenced in various and devious ways, according to the nature of the owner and his or her previous experience.

I would be the last person in the world to recommend that anyone resort to a scheme of deceit to injure another or take advantage of any person in any manner whatsoever. However, I would be one of the first to help certain people scheme to deceive their own egos in order to relieve them of the fear and poverty complexes by which so many people are bound.

One of my students—a life insurance salesman—wears an eight carat diamond ring which serves him as a sort of magic wand while he is talking to his prospective buyers. This man is one of the largest producers for a mutual life insurance company.

Some time ago, he took his diamond to a jeweler to have it reset in a new mounting. The job required a couple of days. During this time, the salesman worked harder than usual, but he failed to make a sale. He said that when he began to talk to a prospective buyer he would look down at his ringless finger and something inside him seemed to say, "He isn't going to buy, he isn't going to buy."

The small voice proved to be right; no sale was made. As soon as he got his ring back, the salesman received six applications for insurance from six interviews his first day out!

Now, as for myself, if I were caught in public with an eight carat diamond ring on my finger, I would feel so self-conscious that I suspect my ego would let me down instead of alerting me for greater action. But I would recommend it for anyone who, like my insurance friend, gets a mental stimulant from an artificial ego booster.

One of the most effective methods for boosting your ego—and everyone needs to have his or her ego boosted—is to select some person as a "pacesetter" whose achievements you would like to equal or exceed. Use that person as a benchmark against which to measure your own accomplishments.

Your marriage partner can become a powerful stimulant to your ego if the relationship is one of harmony and singleness of purpose. The power of such an alliance creates a force that will propel you to success at a speed far greater than you can now imagine.

Your close colleagues can give your ego a tremendous "shot in the arm" if you associate with the right kind of people. Make sure the people around you encourage you and lift you up instead of depressing you and dragging you down.

Your ego needs stimulation occasionally. Use any tricks that work to motivate yourself. If you need a bauble to boost your self-esteem, buy it. As long as what you do doesn't hurt anyone and it helps you, it is the correct thing to do. If you feel good about yourself, it is apparent to everyone you meet. And, remember, the very next person you meet may be the one who can give you a tremendous boost up the ladder to success.

Wake Up and Meet Your Positive Self

Army engineers in Alaska worked feverishly to complete a bridge. The river was frozen solid and the engineers were using the ice to support the central abutments. Failure to get the central beams into position before the ice thawed would be disastrous.

The steel beams had been made at a Pennsylvania mill, which meant a long haul to the site. To make matters worse, exceedingly bad weather had slowed the shipment down to the point at which the engineers had only a few days to complete the job. Finally, the beams arrived. They were hoisted into position and dropped into place only to disclose that they were a few inches too short.

Warmer weather was rapidly approaching and the steel mill was thousands of miles away. An impossible situation? Not to a positive thinker with leadership ability.

An army engineer with such qualities quickly phoned the steel mill and started the wheels in motion for producing beams of the proper length. Someone at the mill also had those qualities of leadership which make the word *impossible* of no importance. The beams were produced with record speed and rushed to Alaska under the direction of two expediters who kept the beams moving night and day under top priority orders.

The beams were unloaded in Alaska, hoisted into position, and dropped into place exactly three minutes before the ice under the temporary abutments gave way. Here was a transaction that was supervised not only by strong-minded individuals but also by a silent partner who always comes to the aid of individuals who know precisely what they want and are determined not to settle for anything less.

There is a power available to people with definiteness of purpose. This power automatically brings to their aid the inexorable laws which give orderliness and definiteness of purpose to the universe of which our little world is an infinitesimal part.

Abraham Lincoln's greatness revealed itself at its highest level when he was faced by problems which would have eclipsed the souls of smaller men. The failures, defeats and adversities of his early life were transmuted into a degree of intelligence which the average man never experiences. Lincoln had that rare trait of being able to turn on more willpower instead of quitting when the going was hard and success was not in sight.

That is the sort of character that makes truly great men and women. Anyone can quit or change his mind by turning his attention to something else when failure overtakes him; this is precisely what most people do under adverse circumstances. Perhaps that is the main reason why there are so many failures and so few successes in life.

You do not see your real self when you look into a mirror. You see only the house in which your real self lives.

If you aspire to the higher planes of success in life, you should become better acquainted with that great, powerful, *positive self* who lives in your body. It can be the creator of all the joys you desire, all the material riches you need for peace of mind and happiness, and it can keep your physical body free from ailments.

This unseen entity that dwells in your body can carry out to the finest detail the instructions you give it, but you must take the initiative and let it know what you want from life. You are a free agent in the eyes of your positive self, and you have been given the privilege of directing it to ends of your own choice.

There are never a great number of "geniuses" who do the impossible during any generation, but wherever you find one, you will have discovered someone who has made contact with his or her positive self and directed it to definite ends in a spirit of perfect faith.

I have had the privilege of working with and knowing intimately hundreds of the most successful men and women this nation has produced during the past half century. Every one of them attained success through the powers of the positive self.

Take possession of your positive self and it will put you on the success beam that you may ride triumphantly to whatever heights of achievement you desire.

The Power of
Mental Attitude

Whatever your mind can conceive and believe, your mind can achieve!

The Creator of all things gave you complete, unchallengeable control over one thing—the privilege of conditioning your mind with any sort of mental attitude you desire.

Your mental attitude gives your entire personality a drawing power that attracts the circumstances, things and people you think about most. This explains why many people go through life as failures—miserable, ill of body and mind, and poverty-stricken; these are the things they attract by the thoughts they permit to occupy their minds.

Scientists have analyzed, torn apart and explained almost every phenomenon except the miracles that the human mind can perform when it is properly conditioned by belief so intensified that it becomes faith and is directed to definite ends.

When we come into this world, we bring with us the equivalent of two sealed envelopes, which are subject to inspection by no one except ourselves. In one, there is a long list of benefits and riches we may attain by the simple process of recognizing the power of our own minds, taking possession of that power and directing it to ends of our own choice with a positive mental attitude. In the other envelope is an equally long list of the penalties we must pay if we neglect—through ignorance, indifference or otherwise—to guide and direct our mind power.

One of our strangest traits lies in the fact that it takes tragedy, failure or some form of misfortune to make us realize the power of a positive mental attitude.

Milo C. Jones of Fort Atkinson, Wisconsin, made only a modest living as a farmer until he was stricken by paralysis. Then he discovered that his mind power was greater than muscle power. His idea for "little pig" sausages made him fabulously wealthy on the same farm, which had previously barely yielded a living. That was the beginning of the Jones Farm products line that today is a household name.

Your capacity to *believe* is your greatest potential asset. But you cannot draw upon it or benefit from it until you form the habit of keeping your attitude positive. It may help to remember that we are only as small as the circumstances we allow to worry us. And no one can make you angry or force you to fear anything without your full consent and cooperation.

Your mental attitude is the medium by which you can balance your life and your relationship to people and circumstances—to attract what you desire.

Our great American way of life and our free-enterprise system are the products of the minds of men and women who *believed* in them and maintained this belief by controlling their mental attitudes. Believers are the forerunners of civilization, the builders of industry, the creators of empires, the revealers of the bounty made available to us by the Creator of all things.

Truly, whatever your mind can conceive and believe, your mind can achieve.

Keep a Positive Mental Attitude

It's often said that the rich get richer and the poor become poorer. My own studies of the principles that make some persons immensely successful and others abject failures bear this out.

The Bible puts it this way: "For unto everyone that hath shall be given, and he shall have abundance; but from him that hath not shall be taken away even that which he hath." (Matthew 25:29)

Possessions are to be used, not hoarded. Whatever we own, we must employ or it will waste away.

Only one thing is permanent in this universe—eternal change. Nothing remains exactly the same for even a second. Even the physical body in which we live changes completely with astonishing rapidity. You can test these statements against your own experience.

When a person is struggling for recognition and to get a few dollars ahead, seldom will he find anyone to give him a needed lift. But once he makes the grade—and no longer needs help—people stand in line to offer him help.

Through what I call the law of harmonious attraction, like attracts like in all circumstances. Success attracts greater success. Failure attracts more failure. Throughout our lives, we are the beneficiaries or victims of a swiftly flowing beam, like the light of a sun, which carries us onward toward either success or failure. The idea is to get on the success beam rather than the failure beam.

How can you do this? The answer is simple. Adopt a positive mental attitude that will help you shape the course of your own destiny rather than drifting along at the mercy of adversity.

Your mind has been endowed with the power to think, to aspire, to hope, to direct your life toward any goal. It is the one and only thing over which we have the complete, unchallenged privilege of control. But remember, we must embrace this prerogative—and use it—or suffer severe penalties. Truly, whatever it is we possess—material, mental or spiritual—we must use it or lose it.

First, clearly define to yourself the position you wish to attain in life. Then say to yourself: "I can do it. I can do it now." Chart the steps you must take to reach your goal. Take them one at a time and you will find that with each success the next step comes easier as more and more people are attracted to help you achieve your ultimate purpose.

Remember, you cannot stand still. You must move upward toward success—or downward toward failure. The choice is yours alone.

Be Optimistic

Optimism is a matter of mental habit. You can learn to practice the habit of optimism and thereby greatly enhance your chances of achieving success. Or you can drive yourself into the pit of pessimism and failure.

Optimism is one of the most important traits of a pleasing personality. But it results largely from other traits: a good sense of humor, hopefulness, the ability to overcome fear, contentment, a positive mental attitude, flexibility, enthusiasm, faith and decisiveness.

Instead of worrying about the bad things that might befall you, spend a few minutes every day enumerating the pleasant events that will happen tomorrow, next week, next month, next year! By thinking about them, you will find yourself laying plans to make them happen! By doing so, you are getting in the habit of optimism.

No great leader or successful person was ever a pessimist. What could such a leader promise his followers other than despair and defeat? Even in the darkest days of the Civil War, leaders on both sides—people like Lincoln and Lee—held faith in better days to come.

Franklin D. Roosevelt's natural optimism breathed a new spirit of hope into a dejected nation in the depths of the Depression. Even infamous leaders—Hitler, Stalin, Mussolini and Mao—rallied followers with such inspiring phrases as "Tomorrow the world," "Nothing to lose but your chains," and "The new Asia."

Can you—living under the finest social, economic and political system in human history—afford to have any less optimism than those leaders?

Remember, like attracts like in human relations, no matter what the rule may be in the physical world. An optimist tends to congregate with optimists, just as success attracts more success. But pessimists breed worries and trouble without speaking a word or performing an act, because their negative attitude serves as a perfect magnet.

Optimism is, in itself, a kind of success, for it means you have a healthy, peaceful and contented mind. An exceedingly wealthy person can be a failure physically, if his constant pessimism has given him ulcers.

Optimism isn't a state of mind in which you throw judgment to the winds in the starry-eyed belief that the future events will take care of themselves. Such an outlook is only for fools. Optimism is, however, a firm belief that you can make things come out right by thinking ahead and deciding on a course of action based on sound judgment.

At the height of the big boom of 1928 (and several others since), there were false optimists who refused to believe that the bubble could ever burst. They jeered the farsighted "pessimists" who warned that the nation was treading on dangerously inflationary and speculative ground. When the bottom dropped out, the "optimists" were caught short. Many lacked the spiritual strength to seek victory in defeat and revealed themselves as true pessimists. Those who had looked ahead fearlessly and honestly had put themselves in a position—by selling stock short and other such devices—to make a killing. They were revealed as the true optimists.

You can be that kind of optimist. Learn to meet the future head-on. Analyze it. Weigh the factors with clear judgment. Then decide upon your course of action to make things turn out the way you want them. You'll find that the future holds nothing you ever need to fear.

Control Your
Mental Attitude

Mental attitude is always at a fork in the path of life. It can travel the path of success or the road of failure. The one thing that can bring us success or failure, bless us with peace of mind or curse us with misery all the days of our lives, is the simple privilege of taking possession of our own minds and guiding them to whatever ends we choose.

Your mental attitude attracts people to you in a friendly spirit of cooperation, or repels them, depending on whether your attitude is positive or negative; *and you are the only person who can determine which it shall be*.

Mental attitude is a determining factor—perhaps the most important one—of what results one gets from prayer. Only prayers that are backed by a mental attitude of profound faith can be expected to bring positive results.

Mental attitude is the warp and the woof of all salesmanship, regardless of what one is selling—merchandise, personal services, sermons or any other idea or commodity. A person with a negative mind-set can sell nothing. He may take an order from someone who buys something from him, but you can be sure *no selling was done*. Perhaps you have seen this truth demonstrated in retail stores where the minds of the salespeople were clearly not directed toward pleasing the customer.

The successful salesman conditions his mental attitude before he comes into contact with his prospective customer by visualizing himself making the sale. He recognizes that if he makes a sale to his prospective buyer, he must first make that sale to himself through his own mental attitude.

Mental attitude controls, very largely, the space one occupies in life, the success one achieves, the friends one makes and the contributions to posterity one makes. W. E. Henley, the poet, must have understood this great truth when he wrote, "I am the master of my fate, I am the captain of my soul." Truly, we may become the captains of our worldly destinies precisely to the extent that we take possession of our own minds and direct them to definite ends through our mental attitude.

Your mental attitude can be controlled by a number of factors, among them:

- A burning desire for the attainment of a definite purpose based upon one or more of the basic motives that activate all human endeavor. The first three of these are love, sex and the desire for financial gain.
- Close association with people who are themselves positive-minded and who inspire you to think and act in terms of a positive mental attitude.

- Autosuggestion, through which the mind is constantly given definite directives until it attracts only that for which these directives call. This procedure should be carried out both silently and aurally to convince the subconscious mind.
- Daily prayer in which you express gratitude for the blessings you already possess instead of asking for more; and requesting more wisdom with which to make better use of your present riches. This habit is perhaps the most important because it strengthens the full powers of your religious belief and can be made to serve whatever ends you choose.

You have within you a sleeping giant whom you direct to perform any service you desire. When you wake up some morning and find yourself on the success beam, you'll wonder why you hadn't discovered sooner that you had all the makings of a big success.

The Value of
Positive Thinking

Is a negative mental attitude barring your way to success? If so, it's time to change.

The negative-minded person accepts any problem or obstacle as insurmountable. The positive person not only finds ways to overcome obstacles, but actually turns them into stepping-stones.

In Louisiana, a large piece of acreage was put up for sale. Only two bids were received, one from a man who owned adjoining land. He bid low because much of the ground was covered with bamboo growth which he thought made the land practically worthless. The other bidder made an offer twice as high. He got the land, cut the bamboo into fishing poles and sold them for enough money to pay the price of the land!

Thus, a positive mind attracts opportunities for success, while negative mindedness repels opportunities—and doesn't even take advantage of them when they come along.

*　*　*

F. W. Woolworth began as a clerk in a hardware store. The annual inventory showed that the store was stocked with thousands of dollars of merchandise that was out of date and practically useless.

"Let's run a bargain sale," he suggested to the owner "and sell off all of this old merchandise."

The owner rejected the idea, but Woolworth was persistent, as people with a positive mental attitude always are. He kept after the store owner until it was agreed that the plan could be tried out with a few of the very oldest items.

A long table was built down the middle of the store and every item on it was priced at ten cents. The goods went so fast that Woolworth got permission to run a second sale, which also went over with a bang.

Then he proposed to the owner that they go into partnership with a five-and-ten-cent store, with Woolworth supplying the management and the store owner supplying the capital.

"No!" shouted the owner. "The plan will never work, because you can't find enough items to sell at a nickel and a dime."

Woolworth went ahead by himself and piled up a fortune and started the great chain of stores that bear his name. In speaking of the transaction years later, Woolworth's old boss said woefully, "As near as I can figure it, every word I used in turning Woolworth down has cost me about a million dollars."

A negative mental attitude carries with it many related traits—fear, indecision, doubt, procrastination, irritability and anger—which repel people and drive away favorable opportunities. A positive mental attitude brings with it faith, enthusiasm, personal initiative, self-discipline, imagination and definiteness of purpose which attract people and beneficial opportunities.

How does one maintain a positive mental attitude? By thinking and acting on the "can do" portion of every plan or purpose and refusing to accept as insurmountable the "no can do" portion that can be found in almost every undertaking.

Let Habits
Work for You

Your every success and failure are the result of habits you have formed. There are two types of habits—those we form deliberately and voluntarily for definite purposes, and those we permit to form by chance circumstances of life through lack of an organized philosophy. Both types operate automatically once we accept them; both are directly controlled by the great universal law which I call "cosmic habitforce."

Cosmic habitforce is the overall controller through which Nature directs all of her laws. Through it, she maintains the existing relationship between atoms, stars and planets, seasons of the year, sickness and health, and life and death. Nature's maintenance is systematic, automatic and orderly. The stars and planets move with perfect timing and precision, each keeping its own place in time and space.

An oak grows from an acorn—always—and a pine grows from the seed of its ancestor. You know that Nature never makes a mistake and grows a pine from an acorn and an oak from the seed of a pine. These are facts you can see. But do you recognize that they do not just happen by chance? Something has to make them happen! That something is the same power that fixes habits and makes them permanent. The Creator permits humanity alone the privilege of fixing their own habits to suit their own desires.

We are ruled by habits, all of us! Our habits are fastened upon us by repetition of our thoughts and acts. Therefore, we can control our earthly destinies and our way of living only to the extent that we control our thoughts. We must direct them to form the habits we need and desire. Good habits which lead to success can be ordered and used by any individual. Bad habits can be broken and replaced by good ones at will by anyone.

The habits of every living creature except humans are fixed by what we call *instinct*. This places them under limitations from which they cannot escape. The Creator not only gave humans complete, unchallengeable control over the power of thought, but with this gift came the means of processing thought power and directing it to any desired end. The Creator has also given us another privilege whereby thoughts are made to clothe themselves in their physical likeness and equivalent— what we think about happens.

This, then, is a profound truth. With it you may open doors to wisdom and live an ordered life. You will be able to control those factors necessary for your success. The rewards available to those who take possession of their own mind power and direct it to definite ends of their own choice are great. But the penalties for not doing so are equally great.

Cosmic habitforce works no miracles, makes no attempt to create something out of nothing, nor suggests what course anyone should follow. But it does help—even force—an individual to proceed naturally and logically to convert thoughts into actions.

When you begin reorganizing your habits and building new ones, start with the success habit. Put yourself on the success beam by concentrating your daily thoughts on whatever you desire. In due time, these new thought-habits will lead you unerringly to fame and fortune.

Think Accurately

Your power of thought is the only thing over which you have absolute control. To use this power effectively, you must think accurately.

Accurate thinkers permit no one to do their thinking for them.

Successful people have a definite system by which they reach decisions with accuracy. They gather information and get the opinions of others, but in the final analysis, they reserve to themselves the privilege of making decisions.

Accurate thinking is based upon two fundamentals: inductive reasoning based on assumption of unknown facts or hypotheses when the facts are not available, and deductive reasoning based on known facts or what are believed to be facts.

The accurate thinker always takes two important steps. First, he or she separates facts from fiction or hearsay that cannot be verified. Second, he or she separates facts into two classes—important and unimportant. An important fact is one that can be used to advantage in attaining your objective. All others are worthless.

It is a tragedy that many people base their thinking on irrelevant hearsay and unimportant facts that lead only to misery and failure. The accurate thinker recognizes that some "opinions" expressed by others are worthless, even dangerous, if accepted as accurate, because they are based upon bias, prejudice, intolerance, egotism, fear and guesswork.

An accurate thinker turns a deaf ear to the person who begins a conversation with the hackneyed expression, "they say," because he knows what he is about to hear will be nothing but loose talk. The accurate thinker recognizes that no responsible person expresses an opinion on any subject unless it is based on dependable facts. This rule would eliminate as worthless much of the so-called thinking of a vast majority of people.

The accurate thinker recognizes that "free advice"—volunteered by friends and others—may not be worthy of consideration. If she wants advice, she seeks a dependable source and pays for it in one way or another. She knows that nothing of value is obtained without consideration.

Accurate thinkers know that emotions are not always reliable. They protect themselves against emotions by carefully examining and weighing them through the power of reason and the rules of logic.

James B. Duke had no formal schooling and never learned to write, but he developed a keen sense of accuracy in his thinking, which made him one of the richest men in the world. He didn't waste time debating with himself over trivialities or unimportant facts. He reached decisions quickly after he had the facts.

One day he met an old friend who was shocked to hear that Duke planned to open two thousand tobacco stores. "My partner and I," said the friend, "have enough trouble with just two stores and you're thinking of opening two thousand. It's a mistake, Duke."

"A mistake!" Duke exclaimed. "I've made mistakes all my life, and if there is one thing that has helped me, it is the fact that when I make one, I never stop to talk about it. I just go ahead and make some more."

So Duke went ahead with his chain of retail tobacco stores which eventually did a weekly business of millions. He left several million dollars to build Duke University, and that was only a small fraction of the wealth he accumulated by his willingness to make quick, accurate decisions, some of which were right.

Elbert Hubbard once defined an executive as "a man who makes a lot of decisions and some of them are right."

Obviously, accurate thinking calls for the highest order of self-discipline, a trait that is very closely related. Prompt and accurate decisions are the most important cornerstones of success in all walks of life. They are not attainable without courageous and honest self-discipline.

Cultivate Creative Vision

You have at your command the power of imagination in two forms. One is synthetic imagination, which consists of some combination of known ideas, concepts, plans or facts, arranged in a new way. The other is creative imagination. It operates through the sixth sense and serves as the medium by which new facts or ideas are revealed. It is also the medium for inspiration.

Thomas Edison used synthetic imagination to invent the incandescent electric lamp by bringing together in a new way two well-known principles. Long before Edison's time, it was known that light could be produced with electricity by applying that energy to a wire and setting up a short circuit. But no one had yet found a way to keep the metal from burning out quickly.

Edison applied the principle by which charcoal is produced, namely, that wood is set on fire, then covered with dirt so that only enough oxygen can get to the fire to keep it smoldering but not blazing. Taking his cue from the principle that nothing can burn without oxygen, Edison placed a wire in a bottle and pumped out all the air. He then applied electricity to the projecting wires and the incandescent bulb was born!

Dr. Elmer R. Gates of Chevy Chase, Maryland, gave us a good example of creative imagination. He had to his credit more patents than Edison. Most of them were perfected by the application of his sixth sense, which he developed to a high degree.

By shutting himself in a soundproof room and turning off all the lights, Dr. Gates managed to eliminate all distractions so that he could concentrate on attaining information he desired. When the information came through by the way of his sixth sense, he switched on the lights and immediately wrote it down. Strangely, sometimes ideas were revealed for which he had not been searching, a fact largely responsible for the great number of inventions he perfected.

Your five physical senses give you contact with the physical world and make available to you its nature and usages. But your sixth sense, which operates through the subconscious section of your mind, gives you contact with the invisible forces of the universe. It makes available to you knowledge you could not otherwise acquire.

The sixth sense of creative vision becomes more dependable through regular systematic use—just as the five physical senses do. Greatly successful people all have some system for conditioning their minds; some do so *without recognizing what they are doing*.

It was creative vision that led to the establishment of the luxurious Fontainbleau Hotel in Miami Beach.

Hotelman Ben Novack arrived in Miami in 1940 with just eighteen hundred dollars and a dream of a beautiful resort hotel which would be known throughout the world for the comfort and relaxation it offered. By judicious management of his meager resources and the enthusiasm with which he conveyed his dream to financiers, Novack put his creative vision to work, and by concentrating on his definite purpose, made his dream a reality.

Clarence Birdseye, a fur trapper in Labrador, once sampled some cabbage that had been accidentally frozen. From the experience, he came up with the idea of merchandising the quick-frozen foods that bear his name.

Are you making your dreams work for you, through creative vision, as Ben Novack and Clarence Birdseye did?

A very effective method of making use of the sixth sense is to write out a clear, concise description of the problem you wish to solve or the objective you desire to attain. Repeat this several times a day in the form of a prayer. The prayer should be founded on faith so definite and strong that you can see yourself already in possession of your objective.

If at first this method does not bring the desired results, keep on trying. Each time, express gratitude as if you had already attained your objective even though it has not yet come into your physical possession.

The master key to success lies in your capacity to believe that you will succeed. Remember, whatever your mind can conceive and believe, your mind can achieve.

Concentration

The most successful people have acquired the habit of concentration on a single thing at a time, instead of spreading their efforts over many fields.

If you meet failure, concentrate on the search for its cause, facing facts honestly, and you will insure yourself against a repetition of the cause.

Do not concentrate on creating an alibi to escape responsibility for failure or on trying to shift the blame to someone else. This has precisely the same effect as a prayer for failure, because you are laying yourself open for a return visit.

Concentration will help you acquire another valuable asset—a dependable memory.

A well-known writer was assigned by a national magazine to write a story based on an interview with Frank Lloyd Wright. The interview lasted for two hours, but the famed architect was annoyed that the reporter made no notes, and demanded to know why.

"I am making notes," the reporter responded, "in a memory that has been trained to do so without notebooks and pencils."

The next day, Wright was handed an accurate transcript of almost every detail in his interview. To his surprise, he couldn't change a word.

The habit of concentration helps you not only to listen well but to remember what you see and hear. The main reason we often find it hard to recall a person's name only two minutes after being introduced lies in our failure to concentrate our attention when the name is first given to us.

James A. Farley is said to have had an almost perfect memory for recalling the names of people he met. He used a system. When he was introduced to someone, he asked the person to please spell his or her name. Or Farley would repeat and spell the name after hearing it, then ask the person if that was correct.

As Andrew Carnegie once advised: "Put all your eggs in one basket. Then stand by to see that no one kicks the basket over." Through such concentration, he developed the United States Steel Corporation.

Any person who attains a high degree of success usually starts off by putting everything they have behind a single objective. They stay on a single track until they get to their destination. After that, they may branch out by setting new goals for themselves.

What about your own habits of concentration? Do you know exactly what you want from life? Do you have a definite plan for getting it? Then your next step is to concentrate on the goal and the plan with such determination that no obstacle can block your way.

Remember, your only limitations are those you set up in your own mind. Concentrate on overcoming them and nothing can stop you.

Progress Calls for an Open Mind

An open mind is a free mind.

If you close your mind to new ideas, concepts and people, you are locking a door that imprisons your own mentality.

Intolerance is a two-edged scythe that on its backswing cuts off opportunities and lines of communication. When you open your mind, you give your imagination freedom to act for you—you develop vision.

It is hard to realize now that less than a century ago there were men who laughed at the Wright brothers' experiments at flight. And it wasn't all that long ago that Lindbergh struggled to find backers for his transatlantic flight. When people of vision were predicting that we would fly to the moon, few doubted that it could be achieved. Today, it is the scoffers that are scorned.

A closed mind is a sign of a static personality. It lets progress pass it by and hence can never take advantage of the opportunities progress offers.

Only if you have an open mind can you grasp the full

impact of the first rule of the science of success: Whatever the mind of man can conceive and believe, the mind can achieve. The person blessed with an open mind performs wonderful feats in business, industry and all professions while the fool with the closed mind is still shouting, "Impossible!"

It would be well for you to take stock of yourself. Are you among those who say "I can" and "It will be done," or do you fall into the group that says, "Nobody can" at the very moment someone else is accomplishing it?

An open mind requires faith—in yourself, your fellow human beings, the Creator who laid out a pattern of progress for us and our universe.

The days of superstition are gone. But the shadow of prejudice is as dark as ever. You can come out into the light by closely examining your own personality. Do you make decisions based on reason and logic rather than on emotion and prejudice? Do you listen closely, attentively and thoughtfully to others' arguments? Do you seek facts rather than hearsay and rumor?

The human mentality withers unless it is in constant contact with the stimulating influence of fresh thought. Those who used brainwashing techniques during war knew that the quickest way to break a man's will was to isolate his mind, cutting him off from the books, newspapers, radio, television and other normal channels of intellectual communication. Under such circumstances, the intellect dies for lack of nourishment. Only the strongest will and the purest faith can save it.

Is it possible that you have imprisoned your mind in a social and cultural concentration camp? Have you subjected yourself to a brainwashing of your own making, isolating yourself from ideas that could lead to success?

If so, it's time to sweep aside the bars of prejudice that imprison your intellect. Open your mind and set it free!

The Blessings
of Failure

Failure sometimes becomes a blessing when it turns one back from contemplated purposes which would have meant embarrassment or even destruction had they been carried out. It often opens new doors to opportunity and provides one firsthand knowledge of the realities of life. It exposes shortcomings and cures vain people of their conceit.

The British suffered grave defeat and failure when Lord Cornwallis surrendered to the Americans, giving the colonies their freedom. But without such freedom, America wouldn't have had the strength to help save the British Empire from destruction during World Wars I and II.

The War Between the States impoverished the Southern states for several decades. But the law of compensation is now balancing the budget on that old score by moving Northern industry to the South so rapidly that the people are receiving compound interest on the war's toll of pride and possessions.

The angel of compensation has a very long arm and

a very sound memory, plus a wonderful bookkeeping system; sooner or later all debts must be paid and all wrongs must be righted, among whole communities as well as among individuals.

I felt that I suffered an irreparable loss when my name did not appear in the will of a wealthy great-uncle who left his fortune to closer relatives. But that turned out to be one of the many great blessings that came my way through defeat and failure. Not receiving any of that money forced me to work out my own economic destiny, and in so doing I was fortunate to have discovered the way to success for other people throughout the world.

Failure in physical health sometimes diverts an individual's attention from the body to the brain, and reveals the real "boss" of the physical body—the mind—and opens wide horizons of opportunity that would otherwise have remained unknown.

Failure usually affects people in one of two ways: It serves as a challenge to greater effort, or it subdues and discourages them from making another try.

The majority of people give up hope and quit at the first signs of failure, before it even catches up with them. And a large percentage of people quit when they are overtaken by only one failure, be it ever so trifling. The potential leader is never subdued by failure but is inspired to greater effort by it.

Watch your reaction to your failures and you will know if you have the potential for leadership. If you can keep on trying after three failures in a given undertaking, you may consider yourself a candidate for a leadership role in your present occupation. If you can keep on trying after a dozen failures, the seed of genius is sprouting within you. Give it the sunshine of hope and faith and watch it grow into great personal achievements.

It seems that Nature often knocks individuals down with adversity in order to learn who among them will get up and make another fight.

The world generously forgives us for our mistakes and temporary defeats provided that we accept them as a challenge and keep on trying, but there is no forgiveness for the sin of quitting when the going is rough.

Learn from Defeat

Every adversity, every failure and every unpleasant experience carries with it the seed of an equivalent benefit which may prove a blessing in disguise.

Failure and defeat are the common language in which Nature speaks to all people and brings them under a spirit of humility so that they may acquire wisdom and understanding.

A wise man once said that it would be impossible to live with a person who had never failed or been defeated in any of his purposes. This same man discovered that people achieve success in almost exact proportion to the extent to which they meet and master adversity and defeat.

And he made another important discovery: The truly great achievements were attained by men and women past the age of fifty, and he expressed the opinion that the most productive years of men and women engaged in brain work were from sixty to seventy.

Abraham Lincoln lost his mother when he was a very young child. "No seed of an equivalent benefit in that," some may say. But his loss brought him a stepmother whose influence fired him with ambition to educate himself and rise in life.

Marshall Field lost his retail store in the great Chicago fire, and with it almost all his money. Pointing to the smoldering ashes, he said, "On this very spot, I will build the greatest retail store in the world." The great Marshall Field and Company, which now stands at State and Randolph streets in Chicago, testifies that there is the seed of an equivalent benefit in every adversity. Sometimes it takes courage, faith and imagination to reveal that seed and germinate it into the full-blown flower of benefit, but it is always there.

Consider, for example, the case of Michael L. Benedum who, at eighty-six, was the world's greatest oil wildcatter with a personal fortune that numbered in the hundreds of millions.

Ask him the secret of his success, and Mike Benedum would tell you, "I learned to keep right on going when things got tough." For example, he had barely made his first fortune when he took some bad advice and lost his shirt.

Benedum turned defeat into victory by learning a prime lesson: to rely on his own judgment for crucial decisions. Consequently, he "kept right on going" to discover new oil reserves that exceeded the total petroleum used in all of history.

Adversity hit him again when he failed in an attempt to find productive oil reserves in the Philippines. Benedum bounced back, saying, "It's all part of the game. You can't find oil everywhere. If you did, there would be no wildcatting."

Our American society is replete with examples of people who achieved fame and fortune by overcoming adversity. Even physical ailments and handicaps need not impede you—as evidenced by Franklin D. Roosevelt, Theodore Roosevelt, Helen Keller and Thomas Edison.

Learn from defeat as did Richard M. Davis of Morgantown, West Virginia, who fought his way up in the coal mining business only to lose everything, including his home and furniture, in the Great Depression. He learned that his reputation, which he salvaged by refusing to go into bankruptcy, was his greatest asset. With this alone he overcame the challenge of adversity and paid off all his considerable debts.

Davis became the president of the Davis-Wilson Coal Company of Morgantown and, in addition to possessing great wealth, was one of the recognized leaders in the fight for international peace.

You, too, can ride the success beam by learning to discover and build on the seed of an equivalent benefit in each of your setbacks.

Two important facts of life stand out boldly. One is that defeat in some form inevitably overtakes each of us at one time or another. The other is that adversity brings the seed of an equivalent benefit, often in some hidden form.

From analysis of these two facts, it is not difficult to recognize that the Creator intends us to gain strength, understanding and wisdom through struggle. Adversity and defeat cause us to develop our wits and go forward.

It is often difficult for us to recognize the potential of an equivalent benefit in our adversities while we are still suffering from the wounds. But time, the greatest of all healers, will disclose them to those who sincerely search for and believe they will find them.

Overcome Fear to Reach Your Goal

Fear is the greatest single obstacle to success.

Too often, people let fear rule all their decisions and actions. They yearn for nothing but security.

The truly successful person doesn't think in those terms. His reasoning is based on creativity and productivity. As President Dwight Eisenhower said, "One can attain a high degree of security in a prison cell if that's all he wants out of life." The successful person is one who is willing to take risks when sound logic shows they are necessary.

All of us suffer from fear. But what is fear? It's an emotion intended to help preserve our lives by warning us of danger. Hence fear can be a blessing when it raises its flag of caution, causing us to pause and study a situation before making a decision or taking action.

But we must control fear rather than permitting it to control us. Once it has served its purpose as a warning signal, we must not permit it to enter into the logical reasoning by which we decide upon a course of action.

Franklin Roosevelt's famous words, "We have nothing to fear but fear itself," are as applicable now and at any time as when he first uttered them during the Depression.

How can you overcome your fears? By looking them full in the face, by consciously saying, "I am not afraid." Then ask yourself, "Of what?" With that one question you have begun analyzing the situation facing you. You are on the road to reason that will carry you around the emotional obstacle of fear.

The next step is to consider the problem from every angle. What are the risks? Is the expected reward worth taking them? What are the other possible courses of action? What problems are likely to be encountered? Do you have all the necessary data, statistics and facts at hand? What have others done in similar situations, and what were the results?

Once you have completed your study, take action—immediately! Procrastination leads only to more doubt and fear.

A noted psychologist once said that someone alone at night imagining he or she hears noises can settle fears quickly. All they have to do is put one foot on the floor. In so doing, they have taken the first step on a positive course of action toward overcoming fear. The person seeking success must force himself in the same way to control his fear by taking the first step toward his goal.

Remember that no one walks the road of life alone. One of the most consoling—and truest—assurances given to us is found in the Bible: "Fear not, for I am with you always."

Faith in those words will give you spiritual strength to meet any situation.

Discipline Yourself
for Success

Benjamin Disraeli, one of England's greatest prime ministers, attained that high station through the sheer power of his will, directed by definiteness of purpose. He began his career as an author, but he was not highly successful in that field. He published a dozen or more books, but none of them made any great impression on the public. Failing in this field, he accepted his defeat only as a challenge to greater effort in some other field. Thus, he entered politics with his mind definitely set upon becoming prime minister of the far-flung British Empire.

In 1837, he became a member of parliament from Maidstone, but his first speech in parliament was universally regarded as a flat failure. Again, he accepted his defeat as a challenge to try once more. Fighting on, with never a thought of quitting, he became the leader of the House of Commons by 1858, and later became the chancellor of the exchequer. In 1868, he realized his definite purpose by becoming prime minister.

There he met with terrific opposition (his testing time

was at hand), which resulted in his resignation. But far from accepting his temporary defeat as failure, he staged a comeback and was elected prime minister a second time, after which he became the great builder of an empire and extended his influence in many different directions.

When the going was the hardest, Disraeli drew on his willpower to its greatest capacity. It sustained him through the emergencies of temporary defeat and brought him through to victory. In summarizing his achievements in one short sentence, he said: "The secret of success is constancy of purpose!"

All too often people quit when the going gets tough, often when just *one more step* would have carried them triumphantly to victory. There is one unbeatable rule for the mastery of sorrows and disappointments, and that is transmutation of those emotional frustrations through definite planning. It is a rule that has no equal.

Your thought habits are subject to your control and self-discipline. They are the only circumstances of your life over which you have complete control. This privilege carries with it a heavy responsibility because it is the one privilege that determines, more than any other, the position in life you shall occupy. If this privilege is neglected by your failure to voluntarily form habits designed to lead to the attainment of definite ends, then the circumstances of life which are beyond your control will do the job for you, and what an extremely poor job it often becomes!

If you make your thought habits to order, they will carry you to the attainment of any desired goal within your reach. Or you can allow the uncontrollable circumstances of your life to make your thought habits for you, and they will carry you inexorably to failure's shore on the great river of life.

Turn on the full powers of your will and take complete control of your life. Your mind was given to you as a servant to carry out your desires. No one may enter it or influence it in the slightest degree without your consent and cooperation. Harness its power and use it to serve your needs.

Freedom of body and mind, independence and economic security are the results of personal initiative expressed through self-discipline. By no other means may these universal desires be assured.

You are where you are and what you are because of your habits of thought!

Stop Making Failures
of Our Children

There is a great deal of talk these days about juvenile delinquency and the problems of youth. I'd like to tell the story of one problem youth and how he was directed into useful pursuits. I was that juvenile delinquent.

My father was a very religious man. There were two of us boys and I was the older, with a mind of my own that defied all my father's efforts to "reform" me. Our mother had died years before.

I liked firearms and had a couple of pistols hidden in hollow trees on our land in the mountains of southwest Virginia. Because of complaints from the neighbors, my father tracked them down and smashed the weapons with a sledgehammer.

I liked mountain music and had a banjo that I played in secret. But my father's religious leanings were opposed to this, too. He hunted until he found the banjo and destroyed it as well.

Dancing was also forbidden. But from time to time I managed to "borrow" a horse after Dad was asleep and attend dances in the village.

As a result of all this, my visits to the family woodshed were frequent and terrible. But each appointment in this shrine of horrors only made me more determined to violate the rules whenever I could. I was well on the way to becoming a complete rebel against all of the regulations of society.

What saved me was my father's decision to marry again. The stepmother he brought to our mountain cabin was a wonderful, kind and understanding woman. She bought me a new banjo and even helped me learn to play it better. From a mail-order house, she purchased two shiny nickel-plated target pistols—one for herself and the other for me. We spent many happy hours together as she taught me to plink at harmless targets instead of at the neighbors' chickens and cows.

Having won my confidence and love by helping me do the things I wanted to do, she set out to direct my energies to better purposes. She obtained a second-hand typewriter and began teaching me how to express my ideas on paper. Finally, she helped me get a job as a mountain reporter for a string of small newspapers. Now I can look back and point to that moment as the most decisive in my life. Is it any wonder that I am grateful to this great lady?

Because of my experiences, I'm inclined to take the side of juvenile delinquents whenever I hear of their problems.

Not all delinquency stems from the same causes, of course. In many cases, however, I suspect it results from excessively harsh rules that are too strictly enforced. And I fear, too, that many parents fail to realize that the boundless energy that leads youth into trouble can be easily directed toward tremendous success. The person who is listless and lazy, lacking the spirit of adventure, is not the one who will achieve great things. Many men and women who attain high places in our civilization are "troublemakers"—free spirits who aren't afraid to defy convention to strike out on new trails, to jar their followers out of lethargy.

If your child is such a courageous, energetic person, be glad. Help him or her learn to channel a forceful character toward success in life. Praise your children for their willingness to try anything. Show them how to learn from their mistakes when they take a wrong turn. Above all, give them your praise rather than your condemnation, for somehow it is human nature for people to live up to the reputation which others give them.

Sorrow Can Be
a Blessing

Sorrow and grief are inevitable in life. They are inescapable. By realizing this fully, you'll be able to roll with misfortune's punches when they come and recover more quickly.

Sorrow can serve a highly useful spiritual purpose. It can break old, unproductive patterns of habit and thought. It can condition the mind to humility. Sorrow is also medicine for the soul and mind, breaking down the many barriers that usually stand between man and the tremendous spiritual forces that lie within him.

The ancient Greeks understood this fully in their presentation of the dramatic tragedies, which were intended to exert a cleansing influence on the souls of spectators.

A strong character is like fine steel that has undergone repeated heating and chilling. Instead of breaking under adversity, it becomes tempered to even greater toughness. It is in times of deep sorrow that Infinite Intelligence reveals itself to us. Prayer becomes most effective, bringing positive spiritual results and solace.

And only by comparison with the depths of misery can we measure our degree of happiness under normal circumstances.

Sorrow may become a mighty power for good when it is transformed into constructive action that changes one's way of life. Under its influence, sinful men have become good, alcoholics have been reformed and vainglorious persons have learned the need for humility. Some who have suffered sorrow and grief due to the loss of a loved one have often gone on to help others in similar circumstances.

In lifting humanity to the highest plane of intelligence, the Creator wisely gave us a capacity for sorrow to ensure that we would use our superiority moderately and wisely. The abnormal man—the dolt, brute, sadist and criminal—may have great intelligence but lack the capacity for sorrow.

If you have a great capacity for sorrow, you also have a great potential capacity for genius—provided you understand sorrow as a welcome source of discipline rather than as a medium of self-pity.

Some of civilization's greatest works of art and science resulted from moments of grief suffered by their creators. Individually, grief helps people grow. Trouble and adversity also serve to bring people closer together, to renew the spirit of helpfulness and unity among people, as they did for the British during World War II, and our own country during times of national crises.

In the depths of sorrow, you will discover immense powers of courage and faith to help you overcome the more usual trials and tribulations of everyday life. You can overcome the trap of self-pity by deliberately seeking out someone with a greater cause for sorrow than your own. By helping him or her to meet it bravely and master it, you will find your own sorrow has melted away in the warmth of your love for others.

Sorrow, like adversity and defeat, brings with it the seed of an equivalent joy. Look for that seed until you find it. Then nurture it, help it develop and turn sorrow into triumph.

Look in the Mirror

My secretary walked into my office early one morning and announced that a homeless person was outside with an urgent request to see me. At first I decided to save time by sending him the price of a sandwich and a cup of coffee, but something prompted me to have him sent in.

I've never seen a more dilapidated-looking man. He had a week's growth of beard and wrinkled clothes that looked as if he had dragged them out from under a rag pile.

"I don't blame you for looking surprised at my appearance," he began, "but I'm afraid you have me all wrong. I didn't come to see you for a handout. I came to ask you to help me save my life.

"My troubles began a year ago when I had a break with my wife, and we were divorced. Then everything began to go against me. I lost my business, and now I'm losing my health.

"I came to see you at the suggestion of a policeman who stopped me just as I was going to jump in the river.

He gave me my choice of coming to see you or going to jail. He's waiting outside to see that I carry out my promise."

The tone of the man's voice and the language he used indicated clearly that he was a man of considerable education. Questioning revealed that he had owned one of the best-known restaurants in Chicago. I then remembered seeing a news account of it being sold at a sheriff's sale several months previously.

I had my secretary get him breakfast because he hadn't eaten for two days. While the food was being prepared, I got the man's entire life story. Not once did he blame anyone for his condition but himself. That was a sign in his favor and one that gave me my cue as to how I could help him. After he finished eating, I did the talking.

"My friend," I began, "I have listened to your story very carefully and I'm deeply impressed by it. I am especially impressed that you haven't tried to alibi yourself clear of responsibility for your condition.

"I'm also impressed by the fact that you don't place blame on your former wife for your divorce. You are to be commended for speaking of her in the respectful way that you have."

By this time, the man's spirits were rising higher and higher. The moment had come for me to spring my plan of action and I let him have it in a way that made it register as I had hoped it would.

"You came to me for help," I continued, "but I'm sorry to tell you that after hearing your story, there is not one thing I can do to help you!

"But," I continued, "I know a man who can help you if he will do it. He is in this building right now, and I will introduce you to him if you wish me to do so." Then I took him by the arm and led him into my private study adjacent to my office and told him to stand in front of a long curtain, and as I pulled the curtain aside, he saw himself in a full-length mirror.

Pointing my finger at the man in the mirror, I said, "There is the man who can help you. He is the only man who can do it, and until you become better acquainted with him and learn to depend upon him, you will not find your way out of your present unfortunate condition."

He walked over closer to the mirror, looked at himself very closely as he rubbed his stubbled face, and then turned to me and said, "I see what you mean, and may God bless you for not coddling me."

With that, he bowed his way out and I didn't see or hear from him for almost two years when he walked in one day, so changed in appearance that I did not recognize him. He explained that he got the help of the Salvation Army in clothing himself properly. Then he got a job in a restaurant similar to the one he had formerly owned, worked as a headwaiter until a former friend met him there by chance, heard his story and lent him the money with which to buy the place.

Today he is one of the more prosperous restaurant owners in Chicago, as rich as he needs to be in money, but richer still in having discovered the power of his own mind and how to use it as a means of contacting and drawing upon the powers of Infinite Intelligence.

Your Source of Power

Of all the great men I have known, Thomas Edison has intrigued me most, perhaps due to the fact that despite his lack of formal education, he became the foremost man of achievement in the field of science.

Edison was far and away the calmest man I have ever known. He had no frustration. He had no fears. He had no regrets about anything or anyone. He had no grandiose ideas of his own importance, but he did have humility of the heart, which made him truly great.

Once when I was talking to him about the ten thousand times he failed in his experiments to perfect the incandescent lamp, I asked him, "What would you have done if you had not finally uncovered the secret?"

With a merry twinkle in his eyes, he replied, "I would be in my laboratory working now, instead of wasting my time talking with you."

Edison knew no such reality as "failure." To satisfy my curiosity about how many failures the average person can survive without quitting and giving up in despair, I once conducted a survey to ascertain the staying power of men and women in the face of failure or defeat.

The majority of the people I polled quit trying when overtaken one time by defeat. A very small percentage of them kept on trying a second time. But by far the greatest number quit even before meeting with defeat because they expected it, quitting before they really started. Needless to say, there were no Fords or Edisons in this group.

I have observed two of the most important facts concerning men and women who are successful in their chosen occupations and those who are not. The successes speak in the future tense of yet unattained objectives which they intend to achieve. The failures speak in the past tense of their defeats and disappointments. I have never known the rule to fail.

There is another trait I have observed concerning successes and failures. The successful person usually speaks in complimentary terms of others who are succeeding.

Envy and revenge are very ugly words. More ugly still is the character of the person who indulges in these emotions. They represent emotions against which the doors of your mind must be tightly closed if you are to enjoy peace of mind.

Close the doors of your mind to everything that causes you anxiety, fear, anger, pain, envy, greed and the desire to get something for nothing. The penalty for failure to close the doors will be the loss of the peace of mind which you are seeking.

If you have been injured by someone, you are face to face with an opportunity to learn whether or not you have within you the makings of greatness. If you have such potential, you will forgive and close the door on the incident. If you do not have the foundation for greatness, you will find ways to strike back at the person who hurt you.

If you do choose the latter course, you will be the most unfortunate of the two, for truly any person who expresses any form of revenge is unfortunate. Revenge is like a boomerang; it often comes back to wound the person who sets it in motion.

Put your anger or hurt behind that same closed door. Remember, no one can make you angry or hurt your feelings in any manner whatsoever without your willing cooperation.

Your state of mind is something you can control completely. And, you may be surprised to learn, after you become better acquainted with this door-closing idea, how easily you can take possession of your mind and condition it for the attainment of any purpose you desire. No one can control the actions of others or the many circumstances of life which tend to make one angry, but you can control your reactions to these actions and circumstances.

Your mind is your own. You are the sole supervisor of its reactions to every circumstance which affects your life. Learn to close the door of your mind and shut out negative reactions if you wish to find peace of mind and prosperity.

Use the
Unbeatable Master

There is a power that comes from within that knows no social caste, no insurmountable obstacles, no unsolvable problems. It is as available to the poor and humble as it is to the rich and powerful. It is possessed by all who think accurately. It cannot be put into effect for you by anyone except yourself.

What strange fear invades the mind and short-circuits the approach to a secret power that can lift a person to great heights of achievement? Why do most people become victims of a negative hypnotic rhythm that destroys their capacity to use the secret power of the mind?

The approach to all genius has been charted. It is the same path followed by all great leaders who have contributed to our American way of life.

Frank Gunsaulus learned how to tap that secret power that comes from within. As a young clergyman, Gunsaulus had long desired to build a new kind of college. He knew exactly what he wanted, but the hitch was that it required a million dollars in cash.

He made up his mind to get the million dollars. A firm commitment based on definiteness of purpose constituted the first step of his plan. Then he wrote a sermon entitled, "What I Would Do with a Million Dollars." He announced in the Chicago newspapers that he would preach on that subject the next Sunday morning.

At the end of the sermon, a strange man whom the preacher had never seen before walked down to the pulpit and said, "I liked your sermon. You may come down to my office and I will give you the million dollars you need." The stranger was Philip Armour, the founder of Armour and Company.

This is the sum and substance of what happened, and the power which made it happen was applied faith—not mere passive faith, but faith backed by action.

Faith, rightly understood, is always active, not passive. Passive faith has no more power than an idle dynamo. To generate power, the machine must be set into motion. Active faith knows no fear, no self-imposed limitations. Reinforced with faith, the weakest mortal is mightier than disaster, stronger than failure, more powerful than fear.

The emergencies of life often bring people to crossroads where they are forced to choose between roads marked FAITH and FEAR. What is it that causes the vast majority to choose fear? The choice hinges on one's mental attitude, and the Creator has so arranged our powers that we each control our own.

Those who take faith's road have conditioned their minds to believe. They have conditioned it a little at a time by prompt and courageous decisions and actions in the details of daily work. Those who take fear's road do so because they have neglected to condition their minds to a positive attitude.

Search until you find that secret power within. When you find it, you will have discovered your true self, that other self who makes use of every experience of life. Then, whether you build a better mousetrap, write a better book or preach a better sermon, the world will beat a path to your door, recognize you and reward you. Success will be yours no matter who you are or what may have been the nature and scope of your past failures.

Give Thanks Every Day

Many successful men and women claim they are self-made. But the fact is that no one reaches the pinnacle without help. Once you have set your definite goal for success—and taken your first steps to achieve it—you find yourself receiving help from many unexpected quarters. You must be prepared to give thanks for both the human and divine help you receive.

Gratitude is a beautiful word because it describes a state of mind that is deeply spiritual in nature. It enhances one's personality with magnetic charm, and it is the master key that opens the door to the magic powers and the beauty of Infinite Intelligence. Gratitude, like other traits of the pleasing personality, is simply a matter of habit. But it is also a state of mind. Unless you sincerely feel the gratitude you express, your words will be hollow and empty, and sound as phony as the sentiment you offer.

Gratitude and graciousness are closely akin. By consciously developing a sense of gratitude, your personality will become more courtly, dignified and gracious.

Never let a day pass without a few minutes spent in giving thanks for your blessings, because gratitude is a matter of comparison. Compare circumstances and events against what they might have been; you will become aware that no matter how bad things are, they could be much worse—and you will be grateful they aren't.

Three phrases should be among the most common in your daily usage. They are "Thank you," "I'm grateful" and "I appreciate." Be thoughtful. Try to find new and unique ways to express your gratitude, not necessarily in material gifts. Time and effort are far more precious, and the amount of these you spend in showing gratitude will be well worthwhile.

Make your gratitude creative. Make it work for you. For example, have you ever thought of writing the boss a simple note telling her how much you like your job and how grateful you are for the opportunities it offers? The shock value of such creative gratitude will bring you to her attention—and could even bring you a raise. As trite as it may sound, gratitude is infectious. She might catch the bug and find concrete ways of expressing her gratitude for the services you are rendering.

And don't forget to be thankful to those who are closest to you—your spouse, other relatives and those you associate with daily, whom you might tend to neglect. You are probably more indebted to them than you realize.

Gratitude takes on new meaning—new life and power—when spoken aloud. Your family probably knows you are grateful for their faith in you, but tell them so—frequently! You'll find a new spirit pervading the household.

Remember, there is always something to be grateful for. Even the prospect who turns down a salesman should be thanked for the time he spent listening. He'll be much more likely to buy the next time.

Gratitude costs nothing, but it's a big investment in the future.

Help in Achieving Peace of Mind

Your mind grows healthy or sick in response to the stimulation you give it, just as your physical body responds to the food you eat. Some of your daily experiences are good for your mental health, and some must be eliminated before they become a deadly poison.

When you have attained peace of mind, your mind will automatically reject every thought and mental reaction that is not beneficial to your welfare. But before you graduate into this desirable command of your mind, you will find it necessary to voluntarily throw off all negative mental influences that you do not wish to become a part of your character. "Throwing off" consists of transmuting negative thoughts into positive thoughts. This is done by simply switching your mind away from unpleasant thoughts and training it on thoughts that are pleasant.

O. Henry's one and only adventure in crime, which resulted in a prison sentence, was transmuted into talent as a writer which made him an immortal in the field of literature.

Jack London's frustrations during the early part of his life were transmuted into novels which made him a national figure in his lifetime and whose stories are still treasured today.

Knut Hamsun, a Norwegian immigrant, failed at everything he tried. Finally, in desperation, he decided to write his story of disappointments in a book which he called *Hunger*. It helped Hamsun win the Nobel Prize for literature and caused the publishers of the world to beat a path to his door. Then riches came in great abundance—sufficient to enable him to retire.

Remember, one's experiences in life—good or bad —are not important in and of themselves. *One's reaction to those experiences is what counts*. By closing doors on those unpleasant experiences, one may transmute them into benefits of great value to one's self and to the world.

Charles Dickens suffered a disappointment in his very first love affair. Instead of jumping off the highest building or taking an overdose of sleeping pills, he transmuted his unrequited love into *David Copperfield*, a masterpiece that opened to him a career that crowned him with glory and riches fit for a king.

It often happens that before we find ourselves, we must undergo a series of reverses, disappointments, defeats and failures. More than likely Harry Truman would have been greatly surprised if, following his failure as a haberdasher, he had been told that one day he would become President of the United States.

It is a fortunate day for us when we discover that there is no such reality as a permanent loss; that for everything taken away, something of equal or greater value replaces it—perhaps something quite different from the thing we lost.

It is an equally fortunate day when we discover that most of our so-called failures and defeats are blessings in disguise, that they force us to change our course in life so that we are led to greater opportunities, greater happiness and greater understanding.

It would have been difficult to sell this idea to Milo C. Jones when he was a healthy working farmer in Wisconsin, but had you told him after he had been stricken with paralysis and had discovered a mind that made him a multimillionaire, he would have listened to you with respect.

Is it not strange that people seldom come to themselves until after they have been overtaken by disaster? Perhaps the Creator planned it this way. There seems to be no other explanation. The richest copper mine in the world was discovered by a miner who had spent most of his life searching for gold. His trusty mule, which carried all of his worldly belongings, including his mining equipment, stepped into a gopher hole, broke his leg and had to be shot. While trying to dig his mule's leg out of the hole, the miner discovered the rich copper ore.

Remember, when frustration of any sort overtakes you, it may be the silent work of an unseen friend who is trying to save you from trouble.

Contentment

The richest man in all the world lives in Happy Valley. He is rich in values that endure, in things he cannot lose—things that provide him with contentment, sound health, peace of mind and harmony within his soul.

Here is an inventory of his riches and how he acquired them:

- "I found happiness by helping others find it.
- "I found sound health by living temperately and eating only the food my body requires to maintain itself.
- "I hate no man, envy no man, but love and respect all mankind.
- "I am engaged in a labor of love with which I mix play generously; therefore, I never grow tired.
- "I pray daily, not for more riches, but for more wisdom with which to recognize, embrace and enjoy the great abundance of riches I already possess.
- "I speak no name save only to honor it, and I slander no man for any cause whatsoever.

- "I ask no favors of anyone except the privilege of sharing my blessings with all who desire them.
- "I am on good terms with my conscience, therefore it guides me accurately in everything I do.
- "I have more material wealth than I need because I am free from greed and covet only those things I can use constructively while I live. My wealth comes from those whom I have benefitted by sharing my blessings.
- "The state of Happy Valley, which I own, is not taxable. It exists mainly in my own mind, intangible riches that cannot be assessed for taxation or appropriated except by those who adopt my way of life. I created this estate over a lifetime of effort by observing Nature's laws and forming habits to conform with them."

There are no copyrights on the Happy Valley man's success creed. If you adopt it and live by it, you can make life pay off on your own terms. This creed can attract to you new and more desirable friends, as well as disarm enemies. It can bring prosperity to your business, profession or calling, and make your home a paradise of profound enjoyment for every member of your family. It can add years to your life and give you freedom from fear and anxiety.

Above all, the Happy Valley man's creed can bring you wisdom to solve all your personal problems—before they arise—and give you peace and contentment.

Not Too Much,
Not Too Little

In order to enjoy peace of mind, you must learn what is enough. You must learn how to acquire just enough—and no more—of everything necessary for happiness.

To become rich in money is one thing, but to become rich in all of the great riches of life, which make for happiness, is something else. Remember, you are not rich in the higher sense of the word unless you have acquired the way to permanent peace of mind.

Money alone cannot bring peace of mind, but it can, and often does, bring anxiety, misery and fear, which make peace of mind impossible to maintain. Money can become either a blessing or a curse, not by the amount you possess but by the way you use it.

When you use money to enrich the lives of others as well as your own life, it may be a great blessing. But when you use it only for selfish reasons, it becomes a curse; you become its slave and are always struggling to get more of it than you need.

Money that builds companies and provides employment for people and products that people want and need should always be a joy to those who control or own it, because work is essential for happiness, for prosperity and sound health. To maintain it, however, other things are necessary also: play, love and worship. These four must be balanced so that you get a definite amount of each in your daily life.

Work serves as a blessing only when it is performed as a form of worship, allowing you to express your talents and collect your dividends each day from the knowledge that your work benefits others. Work performed grudgingly may lead to poor health and a bad disposition.

Ambition for fame, power and money is a great thing, but too much ambition can lead to decay and death. Selfless ambition, based on a sincere desire to be useful to others, is a desirable quality that seldom creates undesirable circumstances; nor does it lead to the loss of any of the greater riches of life.

Mahatma Gandhi was an outstanding example of the application of unselfish ambition. He subordinated his personal desires to the greater purpose of freeing his people. This sort of ambition carries with it great and enduring power, as the fame and memory of Gandhi so well demonstrated.

But remember, the application of ambition, like every other desirable thing, calls for moderation. Too little ambition will condemn you to penury and want. Too much, inspired by the desire for personal aggrandizement, leads to selfishness and greed—never to peace of mind.

We are only temporary custodians of our riches, our lives and the things we use and enjoy most. We may increase our joy only by sharing with others those things and circumstances that bring us joy.

We often pay lip service to the great principle known as the Golden Rule, but few people live it in spirit and deed. Once in a great while some farsighted individual comes into a full understanding of its meaning, applies it liberally in his business or profession, and the world beats a path to his door to patronize him.

"A little bit of myself," said Henry Ford, "goes into every automobile that rolls off our production lines, and I think of every automobile we sell, not in terms of the profit it yields us, but in terms of the useful service it may render the purchaser."

Ford lived by that principle, and it made him one of the most prosperous industrialists the world has ever known. He learned the lesson of selfless ambition quite early in life, and it brought him peace of mind.

The business of living and meeting the problems of life may be either an eternal ordeal or a great pleasure, depending on how you relate yourself to the circumstances of life. Only by planned organization and balance can peace of mind be attained.

When you reach the degree of self-discipline that allows you to fear nothing, hate no one, envy no one, covet nothing you haven't earned and make use of all your experiences to your advantage, a great truth will reveal itself to you. You will realize that your peace of mind is the result of your living by the precept of all things in moderation.

Does This Picture
Fit You?

Frequent, critical self-analysis is necessary to ensure that you are adhering to the principles that can carry you to the heights of success. Perhaps a checklist will help you find the weak points that are impeding you. Try comparing yourself to an imaginary success-bound person—let's call her Mary Smith—and see how you stack up.

Mary has set a definite goal in life for herself and has laid a plan for attaining it within a time limit. In short, she's taken the first and most important step toward success. Have you?

Each time Mary meets a temporary defeat, instead of becoming discouraged, she searches for the seed of an equivalent benefit she can find to turn events in her favor.

Mary lives each day with zest and enthusiasm that make play of her work. She refrains from discussing her troubles with others, knowing that success is bred by the very sound of success.

Moreover, she knows that greater success can be obtained by the group than the individual. She eagerly seeks cooperative alliances in which a free exchange of ideas, talents and energies will more certainly result in reaching the desired goals. She constantly goes the extra mile, giving more than expected.

Mary dresses appropriately, she budgets her income and carefully sets aside some of it in savings and she guards her health.

Above all, Mary maintains a perpetually positive mental attitude. She is convinced of the truth of the first principle of the Science of Success—Whatever the mind can conceive and believe, the mind can achieve—and makes sure that all parties to a transaction benefit by it, that there isn't any winner or loser. Her superior and subordinates admire her because she makes prompt decisions and takes full responsibility for them.

Mary's loyal. She goes out of her way to give compliments and praise—not flattery—where they are due. And she's a likeable woman to be with. She has a sense of humor, and she is thoughtful and courteous. She never uses objectionable language and regards all people as her equals.

Mary tries constantly to improve herself. She knows that good books, good plays and good art can be enjoyed with little expense in libraries, museums and repertory theaters. Most important, she makes steady use of those facilities.

Mary is dependable and prompt. Her word is her bond. Her credit is good because she knows that too much debt is a millstone that would drag her back as she climbs the ladder of success.

How do you compare to Mary?

The Power of Faith

In its simplest terms, faith means action. It is the application of your faith in yourself, in your fellow humans, in opportunities that are available to you in America, and in God—under any circumstances.

The more worthwhile your goals are, the easier it is to follow the principles of success in achieving them. It is impossible not to be enthusiastic and dedicated to achieving worthy and desirable objectives.

I am not speaking of what I suspect to be true, but what I know to be true. This truth is no invention of mine. I lay no personal claim to it except that of having observed its unvarying application in the everyday walks of life for several decades.

If you demand proof positive of the soundness of these laws of success, I cannot offer it except through one witness, and that is you. You may prove it simply by testing and applying these laws for yourself.

If you demand more substantial and authoritative sources, I refer you to the teachings and philosophy of Christ, Plato, Socrates, Epictetus, Confucius, Emerson,

James and Münsterberg, from whose works I have extracted the more important fundamentals. To this I have added that which I have gathered from my own experiences.

Inherent in the principle of applied faith is the sustained application of the Golden Rule in your daily life. For more than four thousand years, men have been preaching the Golden Rule as a suitable rule of conduct, but, unfortunately, the world has accepted the letter while totally missing the spirit of this universal injunction. We have accepted the Golden Rule merely as a sound rule of ethical conduct but we have failed to understand the law upon which it is based.

The law is this: We reap what we sow. When you select a rule of conduct which you use to guide yourself in your transactions with others, you will be fair and just if you know that you are setting in motion a power that will run its course (for good or bad) in the lives of others, returning finally to help or hinder you according to its nature.

It is your privilege to deal unjustly with others, but if you understand the basis for the Golden Rule, you must know that your unjust dealings will come home to roost. The law does not mean merely the flinging back upon you your acts of injustice and unkindness toward others; it goes much further and returns to you the results of every thought you release.

Therefore, not only is it advisable to "do unto others as you wish them to do unto you," but you must "think of others as you wish them to think of you," to avail yourself fully of the benefits of this great universal law.

Your character is the sum total of your thoughts and deeds; it is impossible, then, for you to render any useful service or perform any act of kindness to others without benefitting yourself. It is equally impossible for you to indulge in a destructive act or thought without paying the penalty in the loss of a corresponding amount of your own power and peace of mind.

You are a human magnet. You attract to yourself those whose characters harmonize with your own and repel all others. If you wish to attract considerate, kind, generous, successful people, you must be such a person yourself. The choice is yours alone.

Upon request, the reader may receive an autographed bookplate bearing the signature of the author. Address your request to the Napoleon Hill Foundation, PO Box 1277, Wise, VA 24293, and enclose a large, self-addressed, stamped envelope. With this bookplate you will receive a copy of one of Dr. Hill's famous success essays.

Index

action, two forms of, 43
advancement, earning, 49–
    51, 52–53, 57–58
adversity, overcoming, 68–
    69, 108, 110–11, 122,
    136
    see also struggle
advice, taking, 96
Air Force, U.S., 66
ambition, 141, 142
Americans, 22, 106
American Shirtboard Ad-
    vertising Company,
    45
AON Insurance Compa-
    nies, xi
appreciation of others, 10–
    12, 39, 51, 132–34
Armour and Company,
    130
Armour, Philip, 130

Ashton, John Wesley, 46–
    48
assets, recognizing per-
    sonal, 5–6, 37, 62–64,
    79, 123–25
assistance from others,
    62–64
attitude, mental:
    controlling, 86–88, 130–
    31
    power of, 78–80, 81–82,
    84, 89–91
    see also thought
Ayers, Rufus A., 14–15

Bank of America, 26
Bannister, Constance, 23–
    24
belief, power of, 79–80,
    100, 130
    see also faith

Benedum, Michael L., 110
Berry, Martha, 17–18
Bible, passages from the, 67, 81, 113
Birdseye, Clarence, 100
blessings:
  giving thanks for, 37, 59, 88, 133
  recognizing, 69–70, 106–08, 112, 120–22, 137
brainwashing, 104
Braxton, Lee, 69–70
British Empire, 106, 114
British, struggles of the, 106, 121
Browning, Robert, 23

Capital Airlines, 29
Carnegie, Andrew, 5, 43–44, 54
  philosophy of, 58, 65–66, 102
character, strong, 120
Chicago Boys Clubs, xi
Chicago fire, great, 110
Christ, 145
Chrysler, Walter P., 41–42
Civil War, 83, 106
closed mind, 103–05
Collier, John, 62–63
communicating, 32
compensation, law of, 106–07
concentration, 101–02

conduct, rule of, 146
Confucius, 145
contentment, xiv, 138–39
cooperation, 25–27, 57–59, 60–61, 65–67
Cornwallis, Charles, 106
"cosmic habitforce," 92, 93, 94
creativity, 98–100
Creator, the, 12, 32, 80
  faith in, 104
  gifts from, 4, 45, 78, 93, 121, 130
  intentions of, 111, 137
Curie, Marie, 42

David Copperfield, 136
Davis, Richard M., 111
Davis-Wilson Coal Company, 111
decision-making, 97
defeat, learning from, 109–12, 122
  see also struggle
delinquency, juvenile, 117–19
Depression, Great, 62, 84, 111, 113
desire, xi, 7–8, 24, 87
destiny, controlling, 93
Dickens, Charles, 136
discipline, 121
Disraeli, Benjamin, 114–15
Downes, Carol, 52–53

Duke, James B., 96–97
Duke University, 97
"Dull, Joe," 37, 38
Durant, W. C., 52–53

Eastern Airlines, 66
Edison, Thomas A., 5, 24,
    98–99, 111
  philosophy of, 33–34,
    61, 126, 127
ego, 72–74
Einstein, Albert, 7, 42
Eisenhower, Dwight D.,
    112
Emerson, Ralph Waldo,
    13, 27, 37, 145
energy, personal, 22, 23
enthusiasm, 27–30
envy, 127
Epictetus, 145
Everest, Mount, 24
Eytinge, Louis Victor, 27–
    28

facts, 95–96
failure, 10–12, 78, 117–19,
    126–27
  causes of, 57
  learning from, 70, 76,
    101, 106–08
  see also adversity
faith, 113, 130, 145–47
  see also belief, power of
Farley, James A., 102

fear, overcoming, 112–13,
    130–31
Field, Marshall, 110
First National Bank of
    Whiteville, 70
flexibility, 25–27
Fontainbleau Hotel, 99
Ford, Clara, 26
Ford, Henry, 5, 15, 17–18,
    26, 61, 63
  philosophy of, 8, 127,
    142
Ford Motor Company, 63
Fouche, Glenn R., 39
Franklin, Benjamin, 23
free-enterprise system, 79–
    80
frustration, 137
Fuller Brush Company, 25

Gandhi, Mahatma, 68, 141
Gates, Elmer R., 99
General Motors, 52
genius, 4, 5, 77, 107–08,
    121
goals, 40–42
  achieving, 18, 23, 24
  importance of, x, 1, 3,
    16, 24
  setting, 8, 19, 20–21
God, 145
  see also Creator
Golden Rule, 67, 142, 146
graciousness, 132
Graham, Billy, 32

gratitude, 132–34
Great Northern Railway, 19–20
greed, 141
Greeks, ancient, 120
grief, 120–22
Gunsaulus, Frank, 129–30

habits, 92–94, 115–16
Hamsun, Knut, 136
"Happy Valley," 138–39
harmonious attraction, law of, 82
Heep, Uriah, 26
help, accepting, 62–64
help, offering, 54–56
Henley, W. E., 87
Henry, O., 135
Hillary, Edmund, 24
Hill, James J., 19–20
Hitler, Adolf, 32, 84
Hoover Dam, 69
hopefulness, 19–21
Hubbard, Elbert, 97
humility, 26, 36, 68–70, 109, 127
humor, sense of, 26, 36–37
Hunger, 136

image, 71–74
imagination, 98–100, 103
impatience, 22
Infinite Intelligence, 120, 125, 132

influence over others, 66
influences, negative, 135
initiative, personal, 42, 43–45, 117
inspiration, 58, 59, 98
instinct, 93
International Correspondence School, 56
intolerance, 103

James, William, 66, 146
job hunting, 46–48
Jones Farm, 79
Jones, Milo C., 79, 137
Judeo-Christian philosophy, 68
juvenile delinquency, 117–19

Keller, Helen, 24, 111

leaders, 83–84
leadership, 50, 53, 75–76, 107–08
League of Nations, 26
Lee, Robert E., 83
LeTourneau, R. G., 69
limitations, personal, xi, 6, 101
Lincoln, Abraham, 16, 26, 76, 83, 109–10
Lindbergh, Charles A., 103
Lodge, Henry C., 26

London, Jack, 136
love, importance of, 141

Macfadden, Bernard, 39
magnetism, personal, 31–32
Mao Tse-tung, 84
Maranz, Lee, 2–3
Marshall Field and Company, 110
memory, developing, 101–02
mind, powers of the, 103–05, 116, 125, 128, 129
mistakes, 97, 108
moderation, importance of, 140–42
money, limitations of, 140–41
Mormon Tabernacle, 27
motivation, ix, xiii, 7–9
Munsterberg, Hugo, 146
Mussolini, Benito, 32, 84

Nash, Arthur, 26
Nature, 13, 14, 92, 108, 109, 139
negative thoughts, rejection of, 127–28, 135, 136
    see also attitude
Nobel Prize, 136
Notre Dame, 66
Novack, Ben, 99–100

O'Hancock, Everett, 61
Ohio State Penitentiary, 56
open mind, 103–05
opportunity, 25, 41, 46
    recognizing, 14, 106, 107, 127–28
optimism, xi–xiv, 83–85
others:
    appreciation of, 10–12, 39, 51, 132–34
    help from, 62–64
    helping, 54–56
    influencing, 66
    inspiring, 58–59
    living harmoniously with, 57–59
    working with, 60–61, 65–67

"pacesetter," 73
patience, 22–24
peace of mind, 135–37, 140–42
Pennsylvania Railroad Company, 44
pessimism, 83, 84–85
Philippine Islands, freedom for, 20
Piggly Wiggly Stores, 45
plans, importance of, 1–3, 7, 101
Plato, 145
play, importance of, 141
positive self, 75–77, 131

positive thinking, 81–82, 89–91, 135
see also attitude
power, sources of personal, 126–28
prayer, 12, 59, 69, 86, 120
daily, 37, 41, 88, 100
prejudice, 104–05
prison inmates, xi, 56
problem-solving, 25
procrastination, 43, 45, 113
progress, 103–05
promotions, 49–51, 52–53, 57–58
purpose, 1, 2, 8, 10
definiteness of, 42, 76, 87, 115

Quezon, Manuel L., 20
quitting, 115
see also failure

Randolph, Jennings, 28–29
reasoning, deductive and inductive, 95
reciprocation and retaliation, 67
Remington Typewriter Company, 27–28
reputation, 119
resources, personal, 61
revenge, 127–28

Rickenbacker, Eddie, 60, 66
risks, 112
Rockne, Knute, 66
Roosevelt, Franklin D., 29, 32, 84, 111, 112–13
Roosevelt, Theodore, 111

Salem College, 28
Salk, Jonas, 24
Salvation Army, 125
Saunders, Clarence, 45
Schwab, Charles M., 58
Schweitzer, Albert, 68
"Science of Success," 54, 144
security, 112
"seed of an equivalent benefit," 68–69, 109–10, 111
"seed of an equivalent joy," 122
self-analysis, 143–44
self-confidence, 32, 33–35, 71–74
self-determination, 4–6
self-discipline, 97, 114–16, 142
self-image, 71–74
self-pity, 121–22
self, power over, 82
self-respect, 16, 123–25
self-satisfaction, 7, 16
self, true, 75–77, 131

senses, five, 99
sense, sixth, 98, 99, 100
Sermon on the Mount, 67–68
sharing, 141–42
showmanship, xiv, 38–39
sincerity, 16–18, 30
"Smith, Mary," 143–44
Socrates, 145
sorrow, 120–22
Southern Governors' Association, 53
Stalin, 84
Stayform Company, 39
Steen, Charles, 36–37
Steen, Minnie Lee, 36–37
Stefek, George, 44–45
Stone, W. Clement, xiii
Stork, Butler, 56
strength through struggle, 13–15
struggle, xv, 13–15, 37, 55, 111
    see also adversity
subconscious, powers of the, 34–35, 88, 99
success:
    achieving, 1–3, 60–61, 66, 131
    check list for, 143–44
    creed for, 138–39
    goals toward, 16, 40, 41
    keys to, 9, 36, 49, 54, 60, 68, 97
    laws of, 145
    measuring, 7
    obstacles to, 13, 14, 109, 112
successful people, 10–12
    personal traits of, 1, 4–5, 109, 119
    positive thinking of, 77, 83, 95, 112, 127
    subconscious, use by, 35, 99
    work habits of, 40, 43, 101, 102
Success Unlimited, ix–x, xi

teamwork, 60–61, 65–67
thanks, giving, 132–34
Think and Grow Rich, x
Thoreau, Henry David, 20
thought:
    accuracy of, 95–97
    negative, 127–28, 135, 136
    positive, 81–82, 89–91, 135
    power of, 93, 94, 95, 104
time, budgeting, 11
"Tin Lizzie," effects of, 8
tragedy, 79
"troublemakers," 119
Truman, Harry, 136

U.S. Steel Corporation, 47, 102

vision, creative, 98–100,
103

Wanamaker, John, 8–9,
55
War Between the States,
83, 106
Weeks, Lloyd, 65
Wier, Stuart Austin, 1–2
Wilson, Woodrow, 26
wisdom, 68
Woolworth, F. W., 90
work, value of, 141

World War I, 66, 106
World War II, 66, 106,
121
worship, importance, 141
Wright, Frank Lloyd, 101–
02
Wright, Orville and Wil-
bur, 5, 103

Year of Growing Rich, A,
guide to using, xiii–xv
youth, problems of, xi,
117–19